The Healing Tree

Help for the Hurting

Dr. Al Huba

HUMAC

HUMAC PUBLISHING

FLORIDA · OHIO

For information on all books by Dr. Al Huba
visit his website at www.dralcares.com

.

Published by HuMac Publishing
Designed by Valerie McAninch

CONTENTS

INTRODUCTION

A CAPTIVE AUDIENCE

After spending five years in "*exile*" on Long Island, New York it was a pure joy to return to the land of my love, Alaska. The ministry on the Island, although ordained of God, had taken its toll on me. The pastoral vocation had unfortunately become a grind and after five years my human nature eclipsed my spirituality. The daily negative sensory overload of the city was more than I could endure (or so I believed) so in the spring of 1986 my family and I returned to the Last Frontier. We had gone with some preparation; at least I had a job awaiting me. I was to pioneer a church in the beautiful Matanuska Valley about 40 miles east of Anchorage. The work was slow and arduous, as starting a new church usually is. There were just a handful of people to start with and being of a choleric temperament I had to somehow become busier. I also had to somehow justify the recent 5000 mile move from the relative comforts of New York to the not so comfortable hinterlands of rural Alaska. After some thought I contacted a chaplain friend of mine and asked if he needed any help. That was a foregone conclusion since it would be volunteer chaplain's job and volunteers were scarce. I soon found myself teaching a weekly Bible study at the Palmer Medium Security Correctional Facility. The facility was located in a very scenic and remote area east of Palmer, Alaska in the Talkeetna Mountains. Inmate escapes were rare I learned for even if an inmate was able to scale the 12 foot razor wire fence he had nowhere to go afterwards! If the sub-zero cold of winter didn't get him the ravenous mosquitoes in the summer would.

The prison administration informed me that their greatest need was for me to help the inmates with anger and depression problems. I soon met with my group of 15 men whom I referred to affectionately as my "captive audience". The men, for the most part, were warm and receptive and were all professing Christians. I was blessed to learn that the men had volunteered for the program and were not coerced in any way. For the next 4 months I taught them all that I knew relating to the subject matter and was elated at the results. Feeling good about this, my first accomplishment at the facility, I was ready to move on. After prayer, however, I distinctly heard the Spirit inform me: *"You have only begun your work here. Seek me for your next assignment."*

I returned to my former position and embarked on some general teachings while awaiting further directions from the Lord. Little did I know how quickly the new directions would come!

The men were always punctual for the class usually arriving well before I did. One evening, however, Jimmy, the cook was not to be seen and had not informed anyone, as was the custom, that he would be late. About 15 minutes into the class Jimmy entered the classroom looking a mess. He was covered from head to toe with spaghetti sauce and had only made a cursory attempt to clean himself up. My comment was something like: "Jimmy, you smell divine!" That did not evoke even the slightest smile from him but rather a snarling, "I don't want to talk about it!" My training and instincts told me not to try to push anything so I offered, "OK, whenever you're ready Jim."

After a half hour or so passed I noticed that Jimmy had settled down. I then proceeded to ask if he would like to share with the class what had happened. He then explained how he had labored very hard in preparing the spaghetti sauce, the pasta and all the trimmings. It was also his duty to help serve the food. While he was serving one of the inmates the inmate said to Jimmy that he was ugly, he stank, and didn't know how to cook. Before he knew it he was all over the man. The 25 gallon container of sauce was on the floor and soon the men were rolling in Marinara with meatballs. To Jimmy's surprise he was not disciplined for the incident possibly because of his involvement in my class. I then asked him why he had gotten so angry and he related that it was because of what was said to him by the inmate. I carefully restated the question and received the same answer. I explained to Jimmy that he was not angry over what was said to him but it was something deeper. He thought for a minute then replied that he was angry because what the inmate said to him reminded him of his father. The class and I were stunned and elated at the same time. We all had received an epiphany of sorts. For the remainder of the session all the men shared how their fathers and significant others had put them down when they were younger and even predicted that they would someday end up in prison - another case of "self-fulfilling prophecies."

I left class that day with many things to mull over until our next meeting. In my time of prayer the Holy

Spirit was faithful to show me that the core issue that I was dealing with at the facility was…. **rejection** a subject that I had never thought much about before. Coincidentally, (oh, really) I had begun work on my Masters Degree and what I was to learn experientially from the men at the prison would far exceed all that I would glean from books alone. The finished work (well, almost) that I now present to you facilitators, clinicians, students and clients had its inception in the humblest of places, a prison. May God be glorified by the humble birth of this book as He was by the humble birth of His Son, Yeshua. So I think it only fitting that….

I dedicate this work firstly, to Our Only Wise God and Counselor who makes all things possible, and secondly to the captive audience of 15 men at Palmer Corrections whose candid and unselfish contributions made this book possible. I can only remember a few of their names but I trust that all those names are written in the Lamb's Book of Life.

PASTORAL OBSERVATIONS

Although I had always perceived my primary ministerial calling was that of a pastor, from the inception of that calling I have found myself immersed in counseling. The first church that I pioneered was in Long Beach, Long Island, New York - Messiah Tabernacle. Long Beach was the home of the "Roaring Twenties" crowd of decades ago. The crowd had long ago faded into chronicled memories but the hotels that they once graced still stood as ghosts of a once golden past. Now in a state of disrepair the city fathers were challenged as what to do with the once elegant buildings. The 20's were gone and there was no way to lure the throng back to Long Beach; those days were over.

Located a few miles to the north of Long Beach in the town of Brentwood was the world's largest mental health facility, Pilgrim State Mental Hospital. Built in 1930 and situated on over 1000 acres, at its peak it housed nearly 16,000 patients. Outpatient programs involving independent care and transitional living facilities were always a problem since most surrounding communities didn't want recovering mental patients in their neighborhoods. Since Long Beach was only a few miles to the south and located on the Atlantic Ocean with a beautiful beach and a 2 1/2 mile boardwalk it became a natural attraction for the former patients of Pilgrim State. The slum lords soon seized the opportunity to rent rooms in the old hotels to them using the patients' SSI checks to cover the rent. The rooms were austere at best but at least the people had a place to call home. This is where I met this group of needy people.

As I was taking my customary morning walk along the beach my attention was drawn toward the boardwalk. Built in the 1920's and renovated many times it was now in a state of excellent repair and now venue to hundreds of cyclists, joggers, walkers and those who just enjoyed sitting on a bench and watching the waves roll in. Since I was walking between the boardwalk and the ocean I was able to actually see under it. As I approached for a closer look I felt as though I was entering into a twilight zone. It was eerie. My vision was aided by the bright sunlight streaming through the cracks between the planks on the boardwalk. I was soon able to make out the dim shapes of dozens of people mostly sleeping, some watching the surf. Some were just homeless and some were mental patients attempting to transition back into society. I was intrigued by the fact that they were not **on** the boardwalk but **under** it. The words of the old song by The Drifters, "Under the Boardwalk" seemed to grip my soul. Then the Father spoke to my heart: *"These people have fallen 'through the cracks'."* I had just discovered what would be a large part of my ministry for the next 4 years: ministering to the lost and the forgotten - perhaps more forgotten by the church than by society - those who had fallen through the cracks.

Then they started showing up at our home Bible studies and then, of all things, on Sunday for services. First, there was Shelley, who would open most of our services with a petit and sometimes a grand mal seizure. What a way I thought to start a church, with a woman foaming at the mouth and writhing on the floor! God was at work, however, and Shelley always recovered quickly after a little anointing oil and prayer. The other believers, especially the younger ones, seemed to almost look forward to the Sunday morning deliverances. Shelley was a very faithful attendee at Messiah Tabernacle and seldom missed a service. When she was absent it was usually because of a bout with clinical depression. Once at a Wednesday night prayer service I felt led to pray for Shelley's total deliverance from the seizures and her depression. I asked her if she wanted to be free of her sicknesses she replied that she did. As I began to pray for her deliverance she started to physically manifest the signs of actual deliverance, i.e. heavy breathing, gasping and moaning. But as quickly as it started it ended. When I asked Shelley what was going on, she emphatically replied:" I will never forgive him." When I asked her who "him" was she quickly responded: " My father; he raped me on an elevator when I was 9 years old." Angry tears filled her eyes as she slowly walked away. I was so stunned that words escaped me as my own tears of sorrow slowly ran down my cheeks. Was it possible that this woman's deliverance and healing hinged on her forgiving her father? As I later discovered, it certainly did. God had begun to reveal a very precious truth to me concerning trying to treat people on a surface level that is symptomatic, rather than getting down to the root cause. Then there was Martin who was saved at one of our Friday night church outreaches. This precious soul had suffered moderate brain damage as a result of years of Electro Shock Therapy (EST). Although able to conduct a fairly intelligent conversation he was not employable. Martin was one of the gentlest people I have ever known.

He brought joy to the hearts of many with his oft repeated "*I love you from my heart.*" Prior to coming to Messiah Tabernacle he made frequent trips to a mental hospital for therapy but while a member of the church he needed none. Was Martin a victim of some undisclosed abuse as a child? Perhaps we will never know for sure but we do know that Martin's ability to give and receive copious amounts of unconditional love changed his life for the better. Love did for Martin what no medication could ever do. God was showing me again that treating the symptoms brings no lasting change but dealing with the core issues will. In Martin's case the core issue may have been rejection of some form.

Then there was James, a devout Catholic, who sought me out to help him with depression. He became clinically depressed when his mother died. Depression was only the surface issue; however, the cause was rejection by his father. Marie was my first client suffering from DID, dissociative identity disorder, formerly known as MPD, or multiple personality disorder. Marie manifested 7 alter egos, from that of a schoolteacher to a prostitute. She was successfully integrated only after the core issue was identified - sexual abuse by her brothers when she was a child. That abuse, not dealt with, opened the doors to demonic oppression.

I could cite dozens of case histories of people that I have counseled and/or shepherded over the last 30 years that fit the model previously described; people who have demonstrated various types of illnesses, dysfunctions, and psychoses that when treated symptomatically showed little if any relief until the causes or core issues were uncovered. I won't cite more cases but rather thank God for the experiences and the insights that He has given me in this arena of counseling. It is to you the reader that I humbly offer the following pages. May God help you to sift through what you read and glean some nuggets of truth that will bring healing and deliverance for yourself or for those to whom you minister.

AWH, Clermont, Fl. July 27, 2010

PART ONE

THE ROOT OF THE PROBLEM

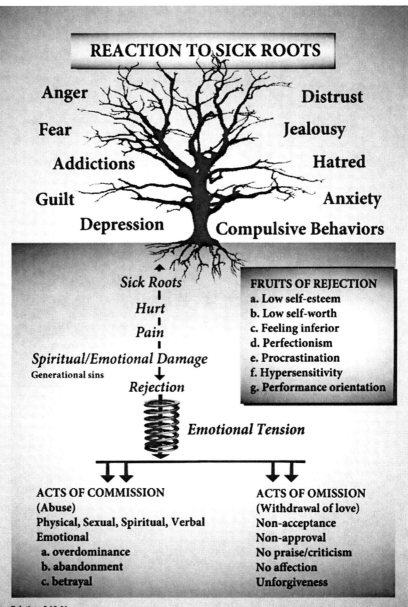

REACTION TO SICK ROOTS

Anger

Fear

Addictions

Guilt

Depression

Distrust

Jealousy

Hatred

Anxiety

Compulsive Behaviors

Sick Roots

Hurt

Pain

Spiritual/Emotional Damage

Generational sins

Rejection

FRUITS OF REJECTION
a. Low self-esteem
b. Low self-worth
c. Feeling inferior
d. Perfectionism
e. Procrastination
f. Hypersensitivity
g. Performance orientation

Emotional Tension

ACTS OF COMMISSION
(Abuse)
Physical, Sexual, Spiritual, Verbal
Emotional
a. overdominance
b. abandonment
c. betrayal

ACTS OF OMISSION
(Withdrawal of love)
Non-acceptance
Non-approval
No praise/criticism
No affection
Unforgiveness

Galatians 5:19-21
Now the works of the flesh are manifest, which are these; Adultery, fornication, uncleanness, lasciviousness, Idolatry, witchcraft, hatred, variance, emulations, wrath, strife, seditions, heresies, Envyings, murders, drunkenness, revellings, and such like: of the which I tell you before, as I have also told you in time past, that they which do such things shall not inherit the Kingdom of god.

THE HEALING TREE

Goodness

Kindness

Love

Joy

Patience

Peace

Meekness

Self Control

Faithfulness

Healthy Roots
Healing

1. FORGIVENESS/RECONCILIATION
2. *Scripture Therapy*
3. *Prayer/Deliverance*
4. *Networking*
5. *Bibliotheraphy*
6. *Addiction Treatment*
   a. *Drugs*
   b. *Sex*
   c. *Alcohol*
7. *Temperament Analysis Profile*

Galatians 5:22-23 KJV 22 *But the fruit of the Spirit is love, joy, peace, longsuffering, gentleness, goodness, faith,* 23 *Meekness, temperance: against such there is no law.*

CHAPTER ONE

❧

SICK ROOTS, SICK FRUITS

Probably most of us have heard a teaching or a sermon at one time or another regarding the bearing of Spiritual Fruits. The fruits that we are referring to are listed in the Book of Galatians, Chapter 6 verse 22: *"But the fruit of the Spirit is love, joy, peace, longsuffering, kindness, goodness, faithfulness, gentleness, and self- control."* Let us remember that these fruits or virtues are not produced directly for God's sake (He isn't hungry) but for the sake of the people that we coexist with here on this planet. They are hungry! These fruits are also produced for God's glory. When people observe us they should be see Christ in the miniature- we should resemble Him. Do not the fruits personify Him? Referring to the believers, the Bible says: *"You shall know them by their fruits."* If there are absolutely none of these fruits evident in the life of a professing Christian then, therefore, there is not enough evidence to convict him of being one. Even a baby Christian should be bearing at least some little green apples - the ripe red ones will come later.

Everyone has their own particular method of bearing these fruits but most focus on **just trying harder**. Who that is sincere about their faith hasn't tried harder? What has been the result for the most part? More frustration? I contend that the challenge here is not one of more effort on the part of the potential fruit bearer but one of examining the root system of the fruit tree. I recommend at this time that you turn to the diagram of the Healing Tree on page 14. Note that the tree is bearing much fruit, the spiritual fruit of Galatians. In John 15 the Father says that it is *His will that we bear much fruit*. What greater ambition can we have but to accomplish God's will in our lives? Now note the sickly tree on page 13. It is bearing sick fruits, "*fruits unto death*" as Romans 7: 5 describes it. Some of the sick fruits are: anger, hatred, distrust, guilt, various addictions, depression, anxiety, fear and compulsive behaviors to name a few. Do these sound familiar to you? Are you captive to any of them? Do you know someone who is? **Fear not**, God is our Strong Deliverer; **trust and obey Him** and He will **set you free!** Hallelujah!

"So, my brothers, you also died to the law through the body of Christ that you might belong to another, to him who was raised from the dead, in order that we might bear fruit to God. For we were controlled by the sinful nature, the sinful passions aroused by the law were at work in our bodies, so that we bore fruit for death. But now, by dying to what once bound us, we have been released from the law so that we serve in the new way, and not in the old way of the written code." **Romans 6: 4-6**

CHAPTER TWO

❧

PAIN

Referring to the Healing Tree diagram you will notice that the first subsurface element that we encounter is **pain**. There has never been a human being that has never suffered some type of pain, whether it has been physical, emotional, or spiritual. Jesus, in fact, suffered all three to a degree that we cannot even imagine. Tuck this thought away for the moment, we will get back to it: Jesus suffered pain; what was His reaction to it?

As a pastor/ counselor for the past 30 years I can assume that when a person comes to me for counsel they are in some sort of pain, usually emotional and/ or spiritual. Although there have been some people in physical pain who have sought my help, especially while I was in the role of a pastor. There are times when the prescription pain killers aren't working and the client resorts to His Divine Healer, Jesus. Usually the client doesn't even realize the extent of the pain unless it's physical. We as a society are better at treating physical pain than the other types. Perhaps it's because we don't associate emotion disorders and pathologies as painful per se. We more often associate pain with a broken toe or a tooth ache. A person is just *"stressed out"*, depressed, worried, angry, afraid, etc. We are more focused merely on how we **feel** rather than categorizing it into the realm of a pain of some sort. As a result we commonly treat the **feeling** rather the **pain** and what is causing it. As a result, through the widely accepted use of psychotropic medications alone, people can begin to **feel better without actually getting better**! Please understand that I am not adverse to the prudent use of medications but I am adverse to its indiscriminate abuse.

Mental health practitioners e.g. counselors, psychologists, and various therapists are at the vanguard of helping the myriad of emotionally hurting people. It can be frustrating at times to see people who desperately need help but make no effort to seek it. The following "dew drop" of wisdom has helped me to contend with that fact: *"A person will remain the same until the pain of remaining the same becomes greater than the pain of change."* Let us move on now to discover where pain comes from.

CHAPTER THREE

❧

HURT AND EMOTIONAL/ SPIRITUAL DAMAGE

GENERATIONAL SINS

Needless to say, all pain has its origin in a particular hurt. The root of that hurt usually lies in the emotional or the spiritual realm. At times it may be difficult to distinguish between the two since there is some overlap in them. As we continue to dig deeper we will find that generational sins are many times at the core of emotional damage. Some of these sins are: drug and alcohol abuse, gambling, anger and rage, pornography, and racism. It is virtually impossible for a child to be exposed to these sins on a regular basis and not be adversely affected and consequently hurt. As depicted in the diagram, generational sins may be the genesis of the hurt or they can be contributory to the problem. In other words, they can be the source of the problem or they can exacerbate an already existing problem. It is not necessary to address further the generational sins and their possible treatment and shall reserve that treatment to other books. It is sufficient to state, however, their effect regarding emotional damage.

Hidden within the heart of every hurt individual is a judgment, conscious or subconscious, against the person who has hurt them, most frequently a father or mother. Many people, for no apparent reason, have an inability to trust God, receive love, to love others, even to love their own husbands or wives or children. They have a difficulty in praying, reading the Bible, and going to church, i.e. connecting with God. The reason for this is that our relationship with our Heavenly Father is primarily shaped by our relationship with our earthly father - especially during the early formative years. Those early hurts and resulting scars incurred from parents can easily be transferred or projected to Father God. Here are some examples:

Possible Parent Types	Attitudes Or Actions	Possible Results
Accidental parent	You weren't planned	Inability to want feel wanted by God & others
Perfectionistic parent	Never good enough	Works hard, never feels accepted by God
Unknown parent(s) God is	No relationship	Intimacy with others difficult
Weekend parent	Not there when needed	Feels unimportant
Too busy parent	Other things take priority	God cares more about others
Broken promises	Didn't follow through	Inability to trust God
"We'll see" parent	False hope	Will God really help me?
Abusive parent	More correction than love	No loving Heavenly Father
Sinful father	In word and deed	Blame toward God

To fully experience the love of God and others and to be able to love others completely we must forgive those who have hurt us. This is covered in Part Two.

GENERATIONAL SINS

Just as certain physical problems can be passed from one generation to another so can certain sins and behavioral and personality tendencies. These are inherited mainly through observation and experience. We tend to become not so much what we have been taught but what our teachers were, i.e. how they acted. Since we are a product of our experiences we tend to reproduce ourselves in our children and in those over whom we have authority. Some notable examples are: A father who never showed his son affection has taught his son to do the same; a daughter dominated by her parents will tend to dominate her own family; a heavy- handed father will tend to produce a heavy- handed son; a child who has been verbally abused will tend to verbally abuse others. Only the healing power of Jesus can deliver a person from the effects of ungodly parenting. Generational sins can be passed on by the law of sowing and reaping. This is one of God's immutable laws that essentially states that whatever you plant by your behavior will be harvested by yourself and others around you. If you do good things, a return of good things will be yours; if, however, you choose to do bad things they also will return, in kind, to you and yours. This is why we have patterns of certain diseases, miscarriages, early deaths, alcoholism, fear, prejudice, mental illness, and perverse behavior.

Lives and families can be destroyed by sins that have not been dealt with in a Biblical way. Unrepentant sin and the consequences of descending behavioral patterns are tools that our archenemy, Satan, will use against us. Remember that he has not come just to harass us but to destroy us and our families. Any clear thinking individual must see this and take appropriate action. **Positionally**, the antidote has been provided at Calvary to cure this problem; however, we must learn to appropriate the cure so as to make it experiential in our lives. Unless this is done, we will most probably be destined to do unto others what has been done unto us; and so the generational wheel will roll on.

CHAPTER FOUR

∾

REJECTION

As I have related in the introduction, I strongly suspected that some sort of rejection was at the heart of the issues that the men in prison had struggled with. Little did I realize at the time that rejection was something that not only affected those men but the scope of it covered a great percentage of the general population. Naturally, people who have suffered from rejection will manifest the fruits or the evidence of having been rejected. The following is a list of those:

- **Low self-worth** - Placing a value on self that purely is an estimate conferred by someone else and has nothing to do with one's true value. This is an under value. Often compares self with others

- **Low self-esteem** - Much the same as low self - confidence. A person having this will be very inhibited and will be an underachiever.

- **Feelings of inferiority** - Sees others as being superior to him. Often compares self with others. Often puts self down.
- **Perfectionism** - Sees things in black and white; there is no middle ground. If there is a defect in something, it is all bad. Things must be done perfectly or not at all.
- **Procrastination** - The cousin to perfectionism. Feels he can't do it right so why not just put it off? Usually has piles of unfinished "to do" projects
- **Performance orientation** - Always adjusting his behavior to please others and to gain their approval, acceptance or affection.
- **Hypersensitivity** - Very "touchy" when approached about certain issues. One must "walk on egg" shells when around them.

Rejection is certainly an emotion but it is also an action. When we say that we reject something it means that we refuse to accept it. When we say that we reject someone it means that we refuse to accept them. This is a very strong action and usually reserved for the most extreme of cases. Few people would confront another and forthrightly say, "I reject you"; however, their other actions toward that person may indicate otherwise. The recipient may then feel rejected even though the word was never used. They, in fact, because of previous rejections may perceive rejection when none may exist. This will become plainer as I now explain the **causes of rejection**:

There are two primary sources of rejection, i.e. Acts of Commission and Acts of Omission:

ACTS OF COMMISSION

Acts of commission are otherwise known as abuse. These abuses are overtly committed against another usually in a fiduciary manner e.g. father or mother toward son or daughter, teacher toward student or pastor toward congregant. Abuse also can occur between husband and wife as well as between siblings.

ABUSE - The following are common types of abuse:

1-PHYSICAL ABUSE - Perhaps the most recognizable and obvious. Can involve slapping, punching, shoving and kicking. More aggravated types can even involve the use knives, guns, clubs and even furniture items. The physical marks left by this abuse are readily observed but the most serious damage may be inward, i.e. emotional.

2-SEXUAL ABUSE - Can involve rape, molestation, sodomy, fondling and other sexually deviant behaviors.

This can all occur within the family or without. If it is within the confines of incest the emotional impact seems to be more severe than if non- incestual. The wounds from this type of abuse runs deep and if untreated will affect one's sexuality whether male or female. Gender confusion is often a result of sexual abuse, e.g. homosexuality and lesbianism. The victim of sexual often has feelings of low self- worth and of being a "throw away commodity.

3-VERBAL ABUSE - Probably the most common of the abuses and least difficult to treat. The features of verbal abuse usually include the raising of the voice, i.e. yelling or screaming in order to gain control. Swearing and cursing may come under this category. Constantly putting another down, denigrating them and speaking in a condescending tone could also be viewed as forms of abuse. Sometimes the clues to verbal abuse are a little obscure. Examples would be: unwarranted silence, e.g. the "silent treatment". Always answering for the other person or incessantly correcting them are other examples.

4-SPIRITUAL ABUSE - Perhaps the most insidious of all the abuses since it affects the body, soul, and spirit. If I had to find a word that captures the essence of this abuse it would **be legalism**. That can be defined as the following:

"Strict adherence to a literal interpretation of a law, rule, or a religious or moral code." When one departs from the **spirit** of the law and adheres to the **letter** of the law he has then descended into the realm of religion. Religion, for the most part is comprised of man -made rules and regulations which are opposed to the formation of **relationships**. Scripture teaches that there is nothing more important than, firstly, a healthy relationship with our Heavenly Father then with our fellow man, especially those within the Body of Christ. The major component of legalism is overt control imposed by leadership over the flock. This control is then maintained by a system of coercion, deception and a radical departure from the leadership style of Jesus whose motive was always driven by love. A pastor must truly love his flock and lead them by love and example, as Jesus does. Sheep are not tough animals; they are easily injured and once injured it may a take a long time for them to heal.

5-EMOTIONAL ABUSE - This type of abuse can be further broken down to 3 forms:

OVER DOMINANCE - This occurs most often in the relationship between the parent and the child. Normally the mother or father by nature should assume a position of dominance. God designed it that way. Someone has to lead, set the good example and set the pattern for the child. That is the role of the parents. This role, however, must not be taken to the extreme situation where the child's natural emotional growth is stifled by not having the opportunity to learn to make their own healthy decisions. Through the learning process the child will naturally make some mistakes, but they must be permitted to do so and suffer the consequences. That is precisely how our Heavenly Father trains us. Even though He is sovereign and omnipotent He is never overly dominant. He always gives us choices while the Son remains our role model. Some parents choose to live their lives vicariously through their children. Perhaps they were disappointed in the outcome of their own early years and want to make up for it by forcing their kids to try to achieve things that they failed to do. Perhaps this why boys are being pushed into sports that they have no talent nor desire for and girls being forced into beauty pageants where they simply do not belong. A child raised in this atmosphere will usually grow up resenting his/her parents and needing help to mature emotionally. Over dominance by a mother and non-assertiveness by a father may be a leading cause of bulimia and anorexia in women. I remember well the client who came to see me while I was in practice in Alaska in the early 1990's. Kim was attractive, blond and in her early 20's. The first session was "just getting acquainted" but by the 2nd session I felt that she was "hedging" and true to my counseling style I asserted myself and suggested we get to the point. She readily acquiesced and shared with me the fact that she was indulging in "purging". She was not familiar at all with bulimia so I had a ready student on my hands. As we talked she informed me that she was living with her parents and couldn't stand it; her mother was too bossy and dad was a "wimp", although she loved him and was close to him. Kim had a good sales job and was quite capable of supporting herself financially. When I suggested that she get out on her own, she froze. "I can't do that!" she exclaimed. When asked why, she had no valid explanation except that she lacked the confidence to move out on her own. Realistically, she had been deprived of the ability to build her own self confidence by a mother who made all the decisions for her. Dad was simply a bystander who gave her little affirmation for fear of what his wife might say.

ABANDONMENT - The dictionary definition means desertion, leaving behind, rejection, or neglect. Abandonment can occur in the physical sense or the emotional or the spiritual. Desertion in the physical sense is the most visible if not the most common. With the high divorce rate that exists it is virtually impossible for the surviving children not to feel abandoned by one parent or the other. Regardless of how fair "shared custody" and "reasonable visitation" rights may appear to the divorced couple, it is never fair to the children. It takes two heterosexual parents to raise a child no matter what pop psychology and the humanists may promote. It certainly doesn't take a village to rear a child either, just two loving, "got it together" parents. A village, on the other hand, only has the capability of raising a "village idiot." Despite the demands and stressors of life parents need to understand that "part time parenting" doesn't cut it, any more than being a part time employee does when we are hired on full time. In short, we need to be there for our kids when they need us (which is more often than we think). There is a myriad of people who have been deserted emotionally. We all have emotions that are God- given and need to be processed in a healthy manner. Parents are usually the chosen coaches to help their kids do this. If a child is fearful he needs to process that emotion. It is not nearly enough to tell the child not to be afraid. First, the fear needs to be validated, e.g." It's ok to be afraid; I'm that way too sometimes. Now let's talk about your fear." Just being there for the person who is experiencing an emotional trauma is enough to allay the negative effects. It's not easy to learn to connect with people emotionally for we are all wired differently. Some of us are just by nature more emotional than others. Communication is the catalyst for connection. We cannot feel the way the other person does but we can learn to empathize with them through caring communication. In marriage counseling a common complaint is, "He or she doesn't care about me." The truth is that the other person does care about them they just have not learned how to communicate while in the sometimes intimidating emotional zone. Quite naturally when one steps away from their uncomfortable zone the other is going to feel abandoned.

BETRAYAL – Betrayal is something nearly all of us have experienced. It can be defined as disloyalty, unfaithfulness, treachery, duplicity, or infidelity. There are no barriers to this nemesis. Neither age nor gender seems make any exceptions. Painful feelings of betrayal run deep and unless healed can cause a life time of problems.

ACTS OF OMISSION

This almost sounds like a contradiction of terms but I assure you it isn't. Overt abuse, the things we actually commit against another individual that we shouldn't have causes hurt and perhaps of equal affect is not doing the things we should have done, i.e. acts of omission. These omissions are also known as a withdrawal of love. The following are some examples:

NON- ACCEPTANCE - To not accept someone is to reject them, which strikes at the heart of subject of this book. When we accept a person we receive them as they are. We may not like what they do or who they are but accepting them as part of God's creation and loving them unconditionally is necessary. I remember a client in Alaska of 15 or so years ago who illustrates the point. He was a successful young lawyer in his mid-thirties who came to me in an extremely troubled condition. His training as a lawyer caused him to be very forthright in his divulgence to the point of actually shocking me. "Dr. Al", he said, I have very troubling thoughts of wanting to kill my step-daughter and I'm really frightened." She loved him and respected him so there seemed to be no logical explanation for this. Upon probing and looking at the roots of his child hood we were able to quickly come to the core of the problem. He explained to me that almost nightly he had a repeating dream or vision. In this vision he saw a woman standing before him dressed in a black robe. Across the front of the robe was a banner that read "Abortion". He stated that he had no idea what the meaning of the vision was. As we talked about his childhood he stated that his father had left the home when he was a young child and that he never felt wanted by his mother. He continued by saying that he felt that his mother had wanted to abort him. As he spoke about his mother he became increasingly upset. We finished the session with me suggesting that he visit his mother who lived out of state and to talk about the issue with her. He reluctantly agreed to do so.

The following week he returned for his counseling session with mixed emotions. He discovered in talking with his mother that she, indeed, had not wanted to bear him and had, in fact, frequently considered aborting him. Although angered at his mother's disclosure he was relieved to finally know the truth. My client even believed that while he was in the womb he knew that he was being rejected. It was eventually determined that the murderous spirit of abortion was passed on to my client from his mother. (This is an example of a generational sin). This sin then was at the heart of his desire to kill his step- daughter. Subsequent therapy was able to free him from that desire and to enjoy a happy relationship with his step- daughter. The antithesis then of being accepted is being rejected which as we have seen can have very serious repercussions.

NO AFFECTION. - It is within all of our natures to desire affection to some degree or another. This affection can be physical, e.g. hugging, stroking, kissing etc.; or it can be emotional, e.g. words of endearment, compliments, or even "good" flirting. When affection is withheld rejection is felt and the fruits of rejection then will surely follow. I can remember a number of years ago reading a news story of a local incident involving the mysterious death of a 2 year old girl. The parents found the deceased in their apartment when they arrived home from work. The subsequent investigation revealed some startling facts. Apparently the parents had left the child unattended each day while they were at work. They left her with a bottle of juice, crackers, a few toys and a TV tuned to the children's channel. This scenario continued for several months. An autopsy revealed no foul play or any other apparent cause for the death. Physically, the baby was in good health. Mental health experts were summoned and after due deliberation a consensus was reached. They agreed that the probable cause of death was neglect; more specifically a lack of affectionate physical contact. The parents were convicted of manslaughter. This is, of course, an extreme case but, nonetheless, illustrates what the withdrawal of love can do.

UNFORGIVENESS - It is very comforting to know that we have been forgiven by God and....by others. When we are forgiven a great weight seems to have been lifted from our shoulders. All too often the words are uttered to a child or another loved one: "I'll never forgive you for that." The damage from that statement is like a double - edged sword; it hurts the non - forgiver as well as the unforgiven one. The result is bitterness for the former and feelings of guilt for the latter. Both, if not dealt with, can result in a lifetime of misery

DISAPPROVAL - This in no way suggests that we need to approve of someone's bad behavior. However, it is still healthy to approve of the person, separating the person from their behavior. By simply saying, "I believe you are better than that" will cause the offender to reconsider his actions. Why not focus on a person's good qualities instead of harping about what is wrong with them? Negativity has never brought about a positive change in anyone. Praise is the antidote to feelings of disapproval and criticism is the catalyst to this form of abuse. Everyone needs to be praised; it is like a medicine for the soul. We are not born with high self esteem and feelings of self confidence. These are imparted to us by the significant people in our lives-chiefly mothers and fathers. We have all heard the phrase "constructive criticism". It's an oxymoron, for criticism is defined as "censure, disapproval, condemnation or denigration". What is constructive about that? We can constructively suggest a change or modification to an idea or action with constructive input and thereby reap positive results. Are there times when we need to be critical of someone? Absolutely, but not in the context of raising children or relationship building. Let us reserve criticism for combating the evil in the world.

CHAPTER FIVE

❧

THE FRUITS OF REJECTION

Persons who have experienced rejection will inevitably manifest certain negative behaviors known as the Fruits of Rejection. They are listed as follows:

1-**Low self-worth** - The person experiencing this may feel that he has little if any value. His perceived worth is based upon what he can do and not on who he is. Many times his "worth" has been estimated for him by people who have been significant in his raising. In order to build himself up, he must tear others down. He must also criticize others to appear better himself. Sometimes birth order will enter in here; e.g. the older son feels left out because the younger son gets all the attention. For purposes of this study self-worth and self-esteem will be considered as synonymous. Feelings of self-worth are not something that we are born with but rather something that is imparted to us and learned usually beginning at an early age.

2-**Feelings of inferiority** - These are closely linked with one's self worth. One who struggles with feelings of inferiority will most often compare his abilities with those of others and fall short in his estimate. This will in turn adversely affect his confidence and assertiveness. Unless checked these feelings will cause the person to live in the pale of always considering himself inferior to others

3-**Perfectionism** - This is the feeling and corresponding behavior that things need to be done as nearly perfect as possible. To some this is generalized to broad areas of one's life but is specific to narrow areas with others. Concerning this person it is better not to even try to do something if he cannot do it perfectly. This person has a tendency to look at all his faults rather than see his attributes. This reminds me of a 24 year old male client of a few years back who was a very accomplished marimba player. He was invited to do a very difficult solo at a high school recital. I listened with amazement at his flawless performance which was met with a standing ovation from the audience. It was not flawless to the performer, however, as he commented after the recital: "Dr. Al, did you hear me miss that note?" He ignored the hundreds of perfectly struck notes and focused on his one error - typical of a perfectionist. This subconscious motive behind this behavior is to elevate one's perceived sense of self-worth by doing something to perfection.

4-**Procrastination** - This is the sister fault to perfectionism. Procrastination is the "fine art" of putting things off that need to be done until "a more opportune time." Those who procrastinate generally have piles of unfinished projects scattered around. The underlying reason why these people tend to put things off is that they are so fearful of not doing something well enough that they never attempt it or they don't have the confidence to finish the endeavor. Procrastinating is an effort to give a person enough time to build up his confidence which rarely comes via this method.

5-**Performance orientation** - Simply put, this takes place when someone tailors his behavior in such a way as to win the acceptance, affection, and approval of others which was probably withheld from them as a child

6-**Hypersensitivity** - One must "walk on egg shells" when around a person who has this problem. Certain subjects are clearly off limits when speaking with them. They can be very easily offended and are usually prime candidates for a healing of damaged emotions.

7-**Cognitive Distortions** - A person who engages in thinking that is self-destructive, negative in nature and based on misperceptions suffers from this. Here are a few cognitive distortions:

 a) Polarized thinking - black or white thinking; things are good or bad; you must be perfect or you are a failure. No gray areas in life.

b) Overgeneralization - Seeing a single negative event as a never-ending pattern of defeat. You come to a general conclusion based on a single incident or piece of evidence. If something bad happens once you expect it to happen over and over again.

c) Mental filtering - Dwelling on negative details and failing to see the positive details. You magnify the negative details and filter out the positive.

d) Disqualifying the positive - Believing that positive experiences do not count or are not valid.

e) Jumping to conclusions - Trying to mind read and foretell the future negatively. You think that you know how people feel about you without having them tell you so.

f) Catastrophizing - Making things bigger that they really are, i.e. "Making a mountain out of a molehill."

g) Emotional reasoning - Acting out your negative feelings as if they were valid reasoning. You believe that what you feel must be true, e.g., if you feel stupid than you must be stupid.

h) Should beliefs - Statements such as: "I should have", "I must have", "I wish I could have." - Trying to remake decisions from the past with the information that you have now but didn't have then. Can we add this to our list of definitions for insanity?

I) Global labeling -Generalizing one or two qualities into a general all- encompassing judgment, e.g., "I'm a loser" etc.

J) Personalization - Seeing oneself as the cause of some negative event and carrying the burden of guilt for it. You think that everything that people say and do is some kind of a reaction to you. You also compare yourself to others, trying to determine who smarter, better looking etc.

k) Blaming - You hold others responsible for your pain, or take the opposite tack and believe that you are responsible for the problems of others.

l) Control fallacies - You feel externally controlled, and see yourself as a helpless victim of fate. The fallacy of internal control has you responsible for the pain and unhappiness of those around you. Later in the book we will learn how to defeat these negative thought patterns.

PART TWO

THE HEALING PROCESS

CHAPTER ONE

≈

FORGIVENESS

&

RECONCILIATION

It is my firm belief that there can be no lasting, permanent emotional or spiritual healing in a person's life without forgiveness on their part. This truth has been born out in countless cases of mine over the last 30 or so years of counseling and pastoring. Our Wonderful Counselor, Jesus, spoke these very important words to us in The Gospel of Matthew Chapter 6 verses 14, 15: "For if you forgive men their trespasses, your Heavenly Father will forgive you. But if you do not forgive men their trespasses, neither will your Father forgive your trespasses." This is surely one of the hardest sayings in all of Scripture for it bears with it not only a duty but a penalty as well. If we forgive others who have hurt us in some way, this being our duty, we will receive the blessing of being forgiven by

God the Father. When we are forgiven we will then no longer bear the burden of the sin of unforgiveness and the emotional weight of it will be lifted. Whether a person is saved or unsaved the emotional load can have the same effect. If we refuse to forgive others we will not be forgiven by the Father and will bear the burden of that sin. I believe that many emotional ills can be traced to bearing the emotional load of not being forgiven by God. Many will ask, "But doesn't the Bible say that if I confess my sins to the Father He will forgive me?" Yes, He will - after we forgive others. Note the words of Jesus in Matthew 5: 23, 24: "*Therefore, if you bring your gift to the altar, and there remember that your brother has something against you, leave your gift there before the altar and go your way. First be reconciled (via forgiveness) to your brother and then come and offer your gift.*" By this we can quickly deduce that our gifts to God can be negated if we are not reconciled to others. The gift to God can be viewed as an external demonstration of our devotion while the reconciliation would ostensibly be an issue of the heart. It is with these mandates of the Lord that I present the following suggestions regarding the subject of forgiveness in an effort to begin healing the damaged roots of the soul.

Let us remember that the object of healing the damaged root system is to, by God's grace, replace it with a healthy root system which will then naturally produce the Galatians 5:22 fruits of love, joy, peace, patience, goodness, kindness, faithfulness, meekness and self- control. Don't forget - Healthy roots, healthy fruits.

Forgiveness and reconciliation are two separate issues; forgiveness being the precursor. Forgiveness is an individual requirement while reconciliation is bilateral, i.e. both (or all) parties must be in agreement for reconciliation to take place. The following steps should prove helpful when seeking to forgive:

1- **Decide** - Forgiveness starts with the decision to be willing to forgive those who have hurt you. Many times we struggle with not really wanting to forgive others. It may surprise you to learn that that is natural, however, in forgiving others we are called to do the supernatural. To quote an ancient sage: "To err is human and to forgive is divine." Only God is divine, but when we ask for His help in forgiving He will impart His divine power of forgiveness to us, thus making it a divine act. When we do not want to forgive it is no time to give up because of that mindset. God is greater than any mindset that we may have. Alright, let us assume that you just do not want to forgive someone. Allow me to ask you this question: Do you want to want to? It sounds like double talk at first but of course it isn't. Most of us would answer that question in the affirmative. Isn't it amazing that even when we do not want to do something God is there to help us to want to; He gives us the desire.

    a) Let us remember that forgiveness is based on a choice not an emotion. The emotion (the feeling of wanting to forgive) will follow the act of forgiveness.

    b) We are not dependent on our own ability and strength to forgive; the same power which provides for our own forgiveness also provides for our ability to forgive others. (Phil 2:13)

2-**Disclose** - Empty out all the stored up hurt to the Father. Specifically verbalize to the Lord how you feel. It is good to let it out to Him. Authentic confession is not grudgingly admitting how we feel but opening up to the father and pouring out our heart to Him. (Psalm 55: 1-23)

3-**Ask** - Ask for God's forgiveness and forgive ourselves for our sinful responses of anger, bitterness, hatred, and unforgiveness. Bring those responses to the Cross and ask

God to forgive you and to cleanse your heart from them with His precious blood.

4-**Release** - Release forgiveness towards others: " I forgive so and so for not loving me or not being there for me or for abusing me." "Father, not only do I forgive that person but I ask that you forgive that person for what they did." If necessary, forgive God for allowing these things to happen to you. Even though God is perfect and cannot do wrong, it may be your perception that requires forgiveness toward God. "Father I forgive you, and please forgive me for blaming you. I recognize it is the thief (devil) who comes to steal, kill and destroy; but you desire life for me in its fullness."

5-**Receive** - Receive the Father's love. "Father, I ask you to fill me with Your Holy Spirit; fill all those places that were filled with anger and unforgiveness. Keep me from self-pity and self- centeredness; renew my mind and keep it stayed on you. I rest in you and I rest in your love."

6-**Bless** - Bless the person or persons who has hurt or offended you. "Father, bless that person and I ask you to love and heal them." Reconciliation is generally a multilateral process where two or more people mutually agree to forgive each other and to move on in a healthy manner. There are times, however, when this may be impossible, e. g., when one or more of the parties has passed away. The remaining party is then left with the choice of simply forgiving from the heart and releasing the other party.

I would be terribly remiss if I didn't share a personal experience regarding forgiveness that has impacted my life even to this day. It was a warm day in the spring of 1958 a week or so from the long-awaited day of graduation from high school. My buddies and I were gathered on the lawn near the entrance of our high school enjoying what was left of the lunch hour. Suddenly I was hit by something from behind me. The blow was centered on my rectal area; the pain was sudden, blinding, and excruciating driving me to my knees then finally onto my back. Everything was spinning and I held back the urge to vomit. When most of my senses returned I was greeted by the hulking form of the class bully glaring down at me in a mocking fashion. I don't remember the words that he spoke to me but I do know that they brought laughter and ridicule from those who I thought were my friends. Their stinging comments were like arrows that pierced my heart and hurt nearly as much the kick from behind.

GREASE

The bully's nickname was "Grease" which came from the appearance of his oily complexion. He was a well- built weight lifter of Italian decent and was both feared and admired by most of the guys. After a few agonizing minutes which seemed like hours to me I was able, without assistance, to slowly rise to my feet. With a new found anger- rooted courage, I half- turned toward my attacker and being careful not to look him in the eye, declared that I would someday kill him. That statement brought an encore of jeers from the group that had now grown to a small crowd. Only I knew that I was serious in my threat for I felt in my heart that I had made a vow that would be kept. I also‾ knew that I was physically incapable of meeting Grease head on in fight; I was a good 6 inches taller than he was but he out -weighed me by 40 or 50 pounds. Since a gun for some reason never entered my mind, there was only one option left for me: I would have to put on some weight in order to beat him up. I believed my boxing skills would then be sufficient to do the job.

My weight- gaining campaign then began in earnest. Over the years because of being under weight, I had accumulated a lot of information on how to gain muscular weight. What I determined to do was pack myself full of calories and hit the weights. My parents' budget couldn't afford the steak diet so I opted for a milk, milk, milk diet. This worked out well for there was a dairy near my home where I could procure a gallon of the protein- packed, unpasteurized, non- homogenized milk each day. I recruited one of my remaining friends to work out with me on the weights each day. He was inspired since he had taken his share being bullied as well. For one year we continued the regimen of one gallon of farm fresh milk and one hour of weight lifting each day with Sundays off. The results were phenomenal! I went from 140 pounds to over 190 pounds of muscle. I was now ready for Grease!

I knew that my adversary would not be hard to find since most of us paid nightly visits to the local drive -in restaurant, Stop-n- Eat. I was there every night for a week but Grease never showed. The word was out that I was looking him. I was not the guy of a year ago; I was big, strong and formidable; just what a bully and a coward like Grease didn't want. He went into hiding and I never saw him again. Revenge, however, was still in my heart, so I took it out on Grease's friends. If they showed up at the drive- in they got a thumping from me and my workout partner. We strangely had turned into bullies ourselves! The last that I had heard was that Grease had joined the Army. Don't think that I wasn't tempted to follow him!

As the years passed the painful memories of that incident faded into the recesses of my mind - hidden but still there. Although I had nearly forgotten the "Greasy Incident" I never realized until years later how it had affected me. Since my late teens I had developed a strong dislike for Italian people. There didn't seem to be any particular reason; I just didn't like them. In 1962 I joined the Army and as fate would have it my company was full of Italians from New York. My encounters with them were not pleasant. Just because they were Italian was reason enough for me to carry an attitude toward them. Fifteen years later things were to change.

While working on the Alaska Pipeline at Prudhoe Bay in January of 1977 I was introduced to the Lord Jesus by my best friend, Steve. A couple of weeks later I formally accepted my Savior and gave my life to Him in a church service in Homer, Alaska. I returned to my cabin in Anchor Point late that night and was promptly convicted by the Holy Spirit that I needed to forgive some people. At first I denied the fact that there was anybody that I needed to forgive. I had hardened my heart to the truth but God was able to soften it. As I agreed to forgive, my enemy of 20 years earlier, Grease, was brought to my mind. Had I really carried unforgiveness for him all these years? God then showed me that I really had and even worse I had hated him! Could it possibly be that the strong dislike for Italians stemmed from my hatred for Grease? I was awake for most of the night forgiving more people than I can recall. When it was over I felt like a totally new person. I felt clean and lighter for the burden of bitterness; hatred and unforgiveness had been lifted from me by the hand of God! God's word tells us not to allow the root of bitterness to spring up within us for it will defile many, i.e., many areas of our lives, especially relationships. I had allowed that root to take hold in my life and it had certainly defiled my relationships with Italians. That root of bitterness that I held for Grease did not confine itself to just him but to all Italians.

In 1978 I was called to the ministry and after finishing Bible School and serving an apprenticeship in my home church in Homer, Alaska I was called to start my first church in Long Beach, New York. As you may have guessed the church was comprised mostly of..... Yes,

ITALIANS! Oh, what a love I had for them. Bring on the pasta, Luigi! I thank you Lord for changing my heart.

CHAPTER TWO

༭

DEFEATING DEPRESSION

UNDERSTANDING THE BEAST

After forgiveness is accomplished the door to further healing is opened. The emotional malfunctions that have resulted from past abuses can now be addressed. One of the most common is that of depression. It would be an over- statement to assume that all depression is caused by some form of abuse but many causes of depression can be traced back to childhood rejection. All of us at one time or another has experienced a period of feeling "blue" or "down." This is a normal part of life. However, if these periods are prolonged they can lead to serious consequences. Depression is not inevitable, but can be avoided and certainly be overcome. Depression is so widespread and common that it has been described as the "common cold" of the mental health field. No one seems to be exempt and no one is immune; every conceivable boundary is crossed. Depression affects the old and young alike, the wealthy as well as the poor, the intellectual as well as the unlearned, the godly as well as the ungodly. It is by far the most common mental/ emotional affliction of mankind and is believed to have caused more suffering than any other single disease. Dr. Harold Bloomfield, in his book, "How to Heal Depression" states:

- One in 20 Americans currently suffers from a depression serious enough to require medical attention, and one person in 5 will have a bout with depression at some time in their life.
- Depression with its various symptoms (insomnia, fatigue, anxiety, stress, somatic pains, etc.) is the most common complaint heard by medical doctors. Two percent of all children and 5 percent of all adolescents suffer from depression.
- More than twice as many women as men are currently being treated for depression; (This may be in part be due to the fact that men tend to deny their depression more than women do.)
- People older than 65 are 4 times more likely to suffer from depression than the rest of the population.

- There are three chief types of depression: Major or clinical depression, chronic depression or dysthymia, and manic depression.

Major depression can be likened to the flu because it clearly has a beginning, a middle stage, and fortunately, an ending. But unlike the flu, major depression lasts longer and if left untreated will usually recur. The recurrence will tend to be more prolonged and will be more serious and debilitating than the first occurrence. Chronic depression is a comparatively low-grade depression that can have a long duration, sometimes lasting for years. Some unfortunate people have suffered from dysthymia for most of their lives. The word dysthymia comes from the root words dys - meaning disorder and thymia meaning mood. It is then a disorder of one's mood

The third type of depression is manic depression and is also known as bi- polar disorder because the sufferer fluctuates from one emotional extreme to another, having extreme highs followed by extreme lows. The lows of depression are usually followed by days or weeks of mania or times of extreme elation, grandiose thoughts and sometimes inappropriate behaviors. The following is a short list of signs to look for if you suspect that someone is depressed:

- Frequent feelings of sadness, the "blues" or downheartedness.
- Recurring spells of crying
- Tendency to overeat or under eat
- Abnormal gain or loss of weight
- Unexplainable fatigue
- Unclearness of min
- Unmotivated most times
- Restlessness
- Loss of hope for the future
- Unusual irritability
- Difficulty in making decisions
- Feelings of not being wanted or needed
- Feeling that life is empty
- Loss of enjoyment in activities.

If you or another can relate to some of the above or a combination of them some form of depression may be at hand. It is no time to despair, however, for there is hope for you. Take heart in the words of Albert Camus, referring to his emotions: "In the depth of winter, I finally learned that within me there lay an invincible summer."

There is little disagreement among mental health professionals as to the cause of depression, i.e. it is due to a chemical imbalance in the brain. However, the causes of the imbalance are certainly open for discussion. Perhaps, at this point a brief discussion of the inner functions of the brain would be helpful. Harold Bloomfield, M.D. and Peter McWilliams are credited as they relate the following:

"The human brain is the most intricate communication center on earth. Ten billion brain cells transmit billions of messages each second. The biochemical messengers are known as neurotransmitters. ('Neuro' refers to the brain cells and 'transmitter' to sending and receiving information.) When neurotransmitters are at appropriate levels the brain functions harmoniously and we tend to feel good. Although we all experience the ups and downs of life, the overall mood is one of well- being, confidence and security. Although there are dozens of neurotransmitters, research indicates that a deficiency in some of them (specifically serotonin, norepinephrine, and dopamine) may be one cause of depression. On the other hand, excessive amounts of neurotransmitters may be the cause of the manic phase of manic depression. Antidepressant medications restore the neurotransmitters to natural levels and bring the brain back into harmonious functioning."

As a mental health professional, I have found that although medications do indeed work wonders in helping the depressed persons get back on their feet, they seldom provide the complete cure. The medications are more of an aid or enabler in the healing process, e.g. as the splint, cast or crutch with a broken leg. The appliance doesn't actually accomplish the healing but rather the body does through its own healing processes.

And so it is with the person suffering from depression, especially the clinically depressed. The antidepressant medication helps the healing process but then the person must adopt a change in life style and in their way of thinking in order to produce any long lasting or even permanent effects. Many factors contribute to common depression. However, the most common is stress. Life for the average person is filled with disappointments, delays, pressing schedules, setbacks, and of course, tragedies such as death, serious illness, injury, or serious financial loss. If we do not deal with these problems appropriately, they can gradually wear us down and weaken us to the point of depression. Often these pressures are beyond our control, contributing to a sense of being overwhelmed and in a hopeless state.

Negative thinking seems to be a chief contributor to depression. It is so strongly rooted in the thought life of some people that it adversely affects virtually every area of their life. Our thinking patterns have a profound influence upon our emotions, our attitudes, and ultimately our will. Thoughts lead to feelings, feelings then lead to actions. Depression is often, simply, a result of wrong thinking.

Depressed people usually only see the dark side of life and have a pessimistic view of life. Life to them is an endless succession of burdens, obstacles, and disappointments which lead to a feeling of hopelessness. Having thus created a picture of despair in their own minds, they therefore reinforce their feelings of despondency.

Our minds are truly part of being "fearfully and wonderfully made." Our mental health will depend, in great part, on how we learn to think. In the words of John Milton: "The mind is its own place, and in itself can make a heaven of hell, a hell of heaven."

CHAPTER THREE

❧

TAMING THE BEAST

MINDING THE MIND

At the risk of oversimplifying, let me state that the healing process for depression can be broken down into two categories: medical and non- medical. These should work in concert with each other and require the cooperation of the respective clinicians. Those who are expert in the mental health field agree that it is usually not an "either/or" choice in treatment but rather both working harmoniously; Although, there are times when the level of depression is such that counseling alone will alleviate the problem.

Whichever the case, it is vital that the patient accept the responsibility for his depression and recovery. It is counterproductive to blame others or circumstances for the emotional downturn. The factors that contribute to the depression- attitude, anger, and negative thinking are all under the control of the sufferer. Many times I will hear a patient complain that they cannot help the way that they feel. This could not be further from the truth. Except in isolated cases where the person has an influencing organic problem, i.e. diabetes, hormonal problems, or brain tumors to name a few, a person's feelings are determined by a single factor -their thinking. In turn his actions then will reflect his emotions. Let's check the cognitive progression here: Negative thinking which leads to negative feelings which in turn leads to negative behaviors, e.g. thinking that I'm a loser, then feeling like one, then behaving like one! Who is in control here? Somewhere there is usually a lie in the mix. Who said that you are a loser? Not God your creator; not your true friends. So it is either your own negative self- talk or it is the enemy of your soul, the father of lies speaking to you. God's help is readily available to us through the use of His Word. A big part of the strategy of The Healing Tree is to bring healing to the troubled soul through the use of God's Word. In this book I will use the term "soul" to refer to one's emotions, will, and intellect.

The "keystone" verse that I use in cognitive therapy (changing the way one thinks) is found in Romans 12:2- "

Do not be conformed to the ways of this world, but be transformed by the renewing of your mind." A short commentary on this verse is as follows: The admonition from the Lord is in command form - "*Do not conform.*" In other words, do not allow yourself to be shaped, as in a Jello mold, to the ways, i.e. moral standards of this world. Being shaped is sometimes a very subtle but insidious process. This is outlined in Psalm 1:1- "Blessed is the man who walks not in the counsel of the ungodly, nor stands in the path of sinners, nor sits in the seat of the scornful. Notice the subtleties of association here: First the man is not to walk in ungodly counsel. The walk can be very casual and seeming harmless. It is a time to get acquainted as with two would be lovers. It is the way of the enemy; "it won't hurt to just walk awhile," He whispers." Nothing will come of it then you can go your way." Nor stand in the path of sinners. Now we have stopped the casualness of walking and have stopped to stand and talk, perhaps to counsel. There is now an exchange of ideas, intercourse. The association deepens now and the unsuspecting victim is drawn further into the web of ungodly counsel. Next we see the person sitting in the way of the scornful. Sitting strongly suggests that they are actually sitting in agreement with the scornful, surely a repugnant thing. Notice not only the declension of the victim but notice those with who he chooses to take counsel with: first it was the ungodly, those who may have some knowledge of God but choose behaviors contrary to what they believe. Next, we have the sinners, those who live an overt life of sin and make no attempt to hide it. Lastly, we have those who are not only sinners, but they are proud of it. They may even mock God and are certainly scornful of Him. God, in his infinite wisdom, tells us not to avail ourselves to their counsel, for, in contemporary terms, "We become like those whom we hang out with." This is an affront to God for we have been called to be holy, different and set apart from the world. Countless times I have had clients who at one time sat under ungodly counsel. This does not necessarily mean that the counselor was ungodly, but his counsel was because it did not line up with the Word of God, the Bible. One does not have to visit a counselor who doesn't know God to receive ungodly counsel; he can merely go to a Christian counselor who doesn't use The Word as his counseling manual. As we can see there are Christian counselors (who follow God's Word) and then there are Christians who are counselors (who do not follow God's

Word). Back to personal responsibility: even if a person has sat under ungodly counsel it is still their responsibility to find godly counsel and sit under it as God leads.

To be transformed means to be radically changed. In this context it means that the mind must be radically changed. Why? Because without this there can be no repentance; for to repent, first of all, means to have a change of mind. My friends, there can be no change of heart without first having a change of mind. One of the most expedient ways to renew the mind is to meditate on the Word. The mind is much like a computer having hardware and software. In our case the hardware, silicon chips etc., has been replaced with "wetware," water and organic material, i.e. the brain. The programs we run are the software or whatever we download into our mind. We can call this the GIGO Principle - Garbage In, Garbage Out. A computer can only generate output based on what has been put into it. Our "wetware" computers function on the same principle. What kind of garbage has the depressed person been feeding himself? "You are stupid, hopeless, ugly, worthless, etc." These are many times the negative messages received in the past from verbally abusive parents now echoing into the present. Then, of course, there are the painful negative garbage memories of the past - shame, anger, fear, bitterness and unforgiveness. Please refer again to the Healing Tree diagram. All this is due to bad programming....from the past. But as a computer can be programmed it can also be reprogrammed FOR A DEPRESSED PERSON to get well and stay that way they must adopt a daily regimen of bible reading and meditation. Don't let the word meditation scare you; it's not the eastern meditation of staring at a candle until you find Nirvana. It is simply reading the Word slowly, thoughtfully and allowing the Holy Spirit to "open" the words to you. As you do this daily, you will find your thoughts and feelings slowly changing from sad and negative to happy and positive. Remember that God is positive so his words to you must be also. You will soon have a new GIGO. "Goodness In, Goodness Out."

THE ANGER VIRUS

Some of the sludge that can accumulate in our memory bank comes from stored up anger which is a main cause of depression. If held inward in our software it will not only use up valuable space but it will act as a virus and contaminate our otherwise positive and healthy files. This mental contaminant must be purged from our minds on a daily basis; the most effective way of accomplishing this by prayer. It would be very profitable to confess our faults to the Lord, especially the sins of anger, bitterness and unforgiveness, knowing that only then are we are forgiven thus lessening the load of guilt and shame.(See I John 1:9)

Is there such a thing as "righteous anger?" I really believe that there is. For example, I believe it is perfectly normal to become angry at the atrocities and unfairness that we see daily. For example, Jesus was so angry at the money changers in the Temple that he turned their tables over and drove them out with a hand- fashioned whip. That was anger! There is no evidence, however, that He harbored anger and bitterness in his heart toward them and He certainly never hated them. There is a secret to Jesus' ability to do that; it is found in John 2:24, 25: " But Jesus did not commit Himself to them, because He knew all men and had no need that anyone should testify of man, for He knew what was in man. We, naturally, are not omniscient as He was, but he gives us a clue here to live by: We must arrive at the point where we entrust ourselves to no one but God. Note that I did not say trust no one but rather entrust ourselves to no one. Entrust means to hand over or to assign, as in to entrust our life to another in the strictest sense. We would certainly be foolish to do that except in the rarest of circumstances. Trust simply means to place our belief in someone or to have confidence in them. See the difference?

Here is what we can learn from this: One of the chief reasons for our anger is that we place unrealistic expectations on other people. We expect others to march to our drum beat when in reality they are listening to their Mp3 player and have their own beat. We expect others to behave in a righteous way when their human nature is totally depraved and prevents them from doing so. It's a little like expecting my little Chihuahua to pull an Eskimo dog sled. She does not have it in her. We will all behave according to our natures, either good or evil. Our good nature, or righteousness, can only be attributed to the regenerating power of God in us. Without that in us we will remain evil according to our sinful nature, much as a room will remain in darkness until the light is turned on.

Back to Jesus and the money changers: Although He was momentarily angry at them and their ungodly behavior; He was not surprised, however, for they knew neither God nor His ways. He certainly did not condone their actions and showed that by His controlled and properly directed anger. We too can then be angry at certain actions and yet learn to separate the action from the perpetrator; much the same as "God hates the sin but loves the sinner." This in no way makes excuses for horrific actions but rather puts things in perspective. Pure water cannot flow from a polluted spring. Certainly this a tall order, but by faith Jesus can stand tall in us if we bow to his example.

IS IT OK TO TALK TO MYSELF?

"When we talk to ourselves through our thinking, we may use a positive, encouraging 'self-talk' tone of voice or a negative, critical tone. The depressed person tends to self-talk very critically, and this condemnation fuels depression. To lift yourself out of your depression, you will need to become aware of your self- talk, and make adjustments to refocus your self-talk into a positive mode."

The Complete Life Encyclopedia

As we can readily see talking to oneself is normal (If you hear audible replies it may be cause for concern, however). So it is not a matter of whether we will talk to ourselves it is how. I will relate a few examples of positive self-talk. These can be used as an antidote for the onslaught of negative thinking:

- God is taking good care of me and meeting all of my needs (not my wants.)
- I am loved with an everlasting love. See Jer.31:3
- I have an abundant life. See John 10:10
- I am being changed and conformed into the image of Christ. See Phil. 1:6.
- I am a new creation. See 2 Cor. 5:17
- I am holy and without blame before God. See Eph. 1:4
- I can do all things through Christ who strengthens me. See Phil.4:13

I listed the positive first because I believe that the positive is always greater than the negative, e.g., *"Greater is He that is in me than he that is in the world"*. (I John 4:4). Here are some examples of negative self- talk that need to be eliminated from one's mind: "I'll never be able to change"; " I always mess things up."; " I don't deserve to be happy". Let us remember that all these negative examples are really lies. They are not based on facts but rather on the way that we feel at the time. **"How we feel is not a sound indicator of the way things really are but is a good indicator of how we are thinking."** (Tommy Newberry)

BRINGING ORDER OUT OF DISORDER

When one is depressed he will almost always feel that his life is chaotic and disorderly. The antidote for that is structure and discipline which is most readily achieved through routine. Some would equate routine with boredom but that couldn't be further from the truth; for it is routine that will keep a person busier and hence more productive (if coupled with discipline).When establishing a routine make sure that you leave ample room for yourself. Get proper rest, exercise, watch what you eat, and find a hobby. Place reasonable expectations on yourself and ensure that your priorities for the day coincide with God's. Yes, God is that interested in you! Here are some suggestions for a good routine.

- Set aside time for daily prayer, Bible reading and meditation, to assure that you maintain a close working relationship with God.
- Make time for building a stronger relationship with your spouse. Include time for fun, talking, and a healthy sex life.
- Make time for relationship building with your children. Train them in the ways of the Lord, pray with

them, get on their level and have heart- to -heart talks with them. Get involved in their life.

- Devote yourself to earning a living but avoid overwork. Follow this order of priority: God and family first, your job or ministry, friends, then self. Notice that I've included God and family together. The reason is that I believe that the two are inseparable. There are too many people who have in error "put God first" and thereby neglected their families.

LAUGHTER, THE HEALER

The Bible states that laughter is good like a medicine. I have come to understand this from not only from a spiritually academic viewpoint but from an experiential one as well. It feels good to laugh and it brings health as well. From a medical standpoint we know that laughter releases brain chemicals called endorphins which relax us, improve our mood and decrease the tendency toward depression. Yes, it is difficult if not strange to laugh when we are depressed. However, it is a matter of acquiring the ability rather than trying to "fake it until we make it". We have not because we ask not and this is a perfect example of that. It is very much in order to ask God for the gift of laughter. Brennan Manning says in his book, The Ragamuffin Gospel, "Don't force prayer. Simply relax in the presence of God... and ask for a touch of folly." Laughter is God's gift to us to help restore a balanced view of life and to handle stress better. It is advisable to learn to laugh at ourselves. The alternative is not so sweet. A few days ago I opened the refrigerator door and was greeted with a tumbling salad dressing cruet. Of course, the cap wasn't on and soon I was wearing balsamic vinaigrette on the front of a clean pair of khakis. A few years ago a few self-denigrating remarks would have rolled out of my mouth. Not this time though; maybe I've finally learned my lesson. I honestly can't say that I laughed out loud over the incident but I did smile as I commented, "Way to go, Al, you make a fine looking salad!" A smile really is the prelude to a laugh.

Part of learning to laugh at ourselves comes from realizing and accepting our humanness. It is easy to place unrealistic expectations on ourselves thus forcing us into the perfectionism mode where all things must be done perfectly. We are all prone to make mistakes and we must learn to be quick to forgive ourselves. After all, God loves us despite all of our shortcomings. Punishing ourselves for our mistakes does no good and only reinforces an already poor self-image. The wise thing to do is to forgive ourselves for being human and to learn from the mistake. (I will place the salad dressing cruet in the refrigerator door instead of on the edge of a shelf.) Those who demand perfection from themselves set themselves up for failure and the resulting disappointment which in turn may lead to depression. Finally, to help produce laughter it helps to watch funny TV programs (you may have to search the archives to find some truly funny ones). I tried a Google search a few weeks ago and discovered some hilarious episodes of "The Amos and Andy Show", " I Love Lucy" and "The Three Stooges." There is nothing like a "Holy mackerel, Andy" or a "nyuk, nyuk, nyuk" to tickle a funny bone! Also try spending time with friends who love to laugh - it's contagious!

Lastly, in treating depression it is sometimes necessary to seek professional help, especially in the case of clinical depression. A professional, such as a psychiatrist, can prescribe the necessary medication that can greatly enhance the treatment. It may also be necessary at times to admit the sufferer to a treatment facility such as a psychiatric hospital. There the patient can receive intensive psychotherapy and be continually monitored and medically treated. They can also be removed from a stressful environment and be protected from suicide attempts. In the facility they may also experience a helpful and friendly atmosphere. There was a time when "Christian counselors" looked at treatment facilities with disdain and even fear believing that therapeutic drugs were "not of God and even of the devil." Fortunately much of that unwarranted disfavor has waned in the wake of sane and unbiased education.

CHAPTER FOUR

ॐ

ANGER ANNIHILATION

Although an active component of depression, I have chosen to treat anger as a "stand alone' subject since many people who have anger problems do not experience depression. Anger, in fact, as we shall see, can be the "fruit" of an abusive past.

The buzzword today in the counseling field is "anger management." If an individual is arraigned in court for any type of violent (or perceived as being so) behavior he will nearly always be ordered to receive anger management counseling. This is also the case for many DUI violators and for many parents who seek parental custodial rights or modifications. It is assumed in court these days that nearly everyone (including the lawyers) needs anger management; perhaps rightfully so.

I prefer not to use the term "anger management" in deference to another term. Why simply manage something when we can rid ourselves of it? If a King Cobra somehow found its way into your home would you try to manage the snake or kill it? All but a few animal rights activists would naturally advocate killing the snake for the safety of human beings. So it is with anger; why try to manage something so potentially dangerous when it can be effectively annihilated; thus anger annihilation. I do, however, realize that there are times when a degree of restraint is required when experiencing righteous anger, e.g., getting angry at social injustices, the murder of innocent victims, etc. Life is full of situations where we will be provoked to anger. That is not the type of anger that we will be addressing but rather the type that is internalized, suppressed, and sometimes even subconscious. It is the kind of anger that many times cannot be explained but rather felt. It lingers, festers, hurts self and the ones we love.

CASE HISTORY #1- THE GANG LEADER

A couple of years ago a 48 year old former pastor came to me for court ordered anger management counseling. This man had threatened an employee of a liquor store with a wine bottle for allegedly stalking his 18 year old daughter. Upon his own admission, the acting out of this offense was out of character for him but the feelings surrounding the incident were not. In other words, there were times when he would feel very angry over a situation but he possessed enough godly restraint to keep him from acting out his feelings. But this particular time he could not restrain himself. He related to me that he had reported the alleged stalking of his daughter to the local police on several occasions to no avail. In an effort to "protect" his daughter he took things into his own hands. I asked him if it was his custom to take things into his own hands and he replied in the affirmative. The client was a former New York street gang member and he related dozens of stories relating to his days in the streets. After much praying and prodding it was deduced by the counselor that this former pastor was still heavily influenced by his own "gang mentality", e.g., taking things into one's own hands since "I got no satisfaction" from the police. Further examination by the counselor revealed that the client had transferred much of this gang mentality/attitude into the home where it caused much trouble with his family. If the family honored him as the "gang leader" things went smoothly, if not, there was a price to pay.

Subsequent sessions revealed that the client harbored feelings of unforgiveness and bitterness toward his father. When asked why he felt this way toward his father he explained that his father always favored his younger brother over him. It seemed as though the younger brother was an athlete and my client was not. Since the father was an avid sports fan he naturally gravitated toward the younger brother. The father was still living and the counselee reported that he and his father talked frequently on the phone and things were OK. When asked if he had fully forgiven his father he replied that he did, however there was still tension between the two. After talking more about the subject the man revealed that he was still hurt by what he felt was a lost childhood because his father spent very little time with him in comparison to his brother.

There are a couple of points I want us to consider here: Firstly, let us look at where the root of the anger began with this client. No doubt it lay with the feelings of jealousy, unforgiveness, and bitterness that he held toward his dad. This then became a fertile breeding ground for what would become volatile anger. When he finally forgave his father and was wholly reconciled, the anger diminished (although not annihilated). Secondly, the client had to deal with his "gang mentality", which was part of his learned behavior. This mentality was demonstrated through various forms of anger all designed to gain control in various situations. He related that the only way for a gang to gain and maintain control in the streets was through force, intimidation, manipulation and coercion, all behaviors that he continued to use, and all fueled by his anger. Although this client did make progress in managing his anger he never reached the point of annihilating it as he struggles to abandon his gang mindset. To do so would mean a loss of perceived control, something that he continues to grapple with.

CASE HISTORY #2- LIFE IS NOT FAIR

For those of us who have trodden the path of life for a quintet of decades or more we can arrive at one conclusion with absolute certainty- life is not fair. Yes, God is always fair but we live on the "down side of the fall" and life is not what it was originally designed to be. When sin entered the world through our first parents the ideal world was then turned on its ear. God was not surprised by this and somehow always had a contingency plan: Jesus the Great Equalizer. He has a way of making things fair even when life isn't. We will have to wait for Heaven to have everything made perfectly clear (as if we will care once we are there). It is superbly comforting to rehearse Romans 8:28 when life seems to be unfair: "All things work together toward good for those who love God and are the called according to His purpose. Note the word toward". We may not see the culmination of what His goodness is working out, but we know that all things are being arranged to bring about an ultimate good in our life. I can think of many examples written on the pages of my memory but one seems to stand out above the others at this point; probably since it is the most recent. Rex was referred to me by a friend of mine who is a vocational therapist. Although he had a strong handshake it belied the fact that he was physically and mentally handicapped. I realize that the word "handicapped" is not politically correct but I use it anyway since it is an accurately descriptive word; not disabled but handicapped in the sense that this man this man can no longer do many of the things he used to do , physically and mentally. However, by the grace of God, he is able to do things now that he could never do before. For instance, he can pray like never before; he can relate to people; he knows God much better now, and perhaps most importantly, Rex cares about the needs of others and will be able to help them.

In 1998 while in his early 20's he was returning to Florida with his fiancé from a trip to North Carolina. He became drowsy while driving and handed the chore to his fiancé who was tired as well. Her efforts to fight off the urge to sleep failed and she drove the pick up onto the medial strip where the vehicle proceeded to flip over 5 times. Miraculously, she escaped without injury but Rex suffered a severe head trauma which left him in a coma for two weeks. The prognosis was not good; the doctors implied that he would live in a vegetative state. God obviously had other plans for Rex. The road to recovery has been a long one; one that will continue for a life time. He had to learn to talk and walk again. Slowly his cognitive and motor skills have returned to the point where he is highly functional... and employable. Rex admits to having been angry at God and in his bitterness asking God the unanswerable question: "Why?" Did Rex feel like his turn of events at such a young age was unfair? Absolutely! As the days turned to months and the months into years the question was never directly answered. He has however, come to experience God's love and hand upon his life. Rex no longer asks why but rather thanks God for being able to serve Him in a most unusual way. He realizes that love and compassion for others is a gift from God and many times is especially reserved for those who have been hurt the greatest. Is life unfair? Not for Rex and a multitude of others who entrust their lives to the Great Equalizer, Jesus Christ. In Him life can be fair.

The names and/ or events in the case histories may have been slightly changed to protect the confidentiality of the persons.

CLOSING REMARKS ON ANGER

I can summarize this section on anger this way:

1-Frequently anger can be traced back to having an unforgiving attitude toward someone who has hurt us in the past. This attitude is then transferred to many innocent and unsuspecting people in our lives. We, in essence, are taking our hurt and pain of the past out on them. Only forgiveness of the past can change that.

2-Anger can come from a constant sense of disappointment. Being human we all have a right to expect something from people. The problem arises when we expect from others what they are not willing or are unable to give; thus the disappointment. For example, we can be commuting into the city at rush hour and expect everything to go smoothly, failing to realize that everyone else on the road has faults, moods, and weaknesses just like we do. "Don't we unrealistically expect everyone to have it together for the commute?" Perhaps the "moron" who just cut me off is having an awful migraine and can hardly see and is hoping he can just make it to work. How about "old pokey" in front of you who is barely driving the speed limit? You didn't know that he is 85 and is recovering from open heart surgery. He is so happy that he is alive and still able to drive! Want to rain on his parade? Your patience with that woman driver a few cars ahead of you is wearing thin. She seems to be driving erratically, and isn't paying attention to the road. Her husband just this morning informed her that he has found someone else but not to worry he'll still take care of her and the three young kids. Want to try to focus on driving while carrying that burden my friend? Go ahead and expect but don't be disappointed when what we receive is what we just gave to someone else yesterday. It might be a good idea to adjust the rearview mirror to see both the traffic behind us and our own face too. "Judge ye not lest ye be judged."

3-Anger can stem from a sense of injustice. We are all surrounded by a myriad of social injustices which will probably grow worse as our society continues to decay. This social decay is but a result of society drifting away from God's moral law. In a country founded upon His Laws isn't it hard to fathom that there are those who would cut our ties with the Father by removing the Ten Commandments from the public domain? Our only hope is in God who hears the prayers of the righteous. The Birkat HaDin (restoration of justice) is a blessing taken from the Jewish Amidah which supplicates: "Restore our judges as at early times, and advisors as there once were. Remove our sorrows and troubles: we want You Adonai, to rule over us with kindness and compassion and to justify us in justice. 'Blessed are you, Lord, the King who loves righteousness and justice.'

CHAPTER FIVE

∽

BOUNDARIES

WHO NEEDS THEM?

The very word "boundary" connotes something negative to most people. But in reality a boundary is very positive and necessary. A boundary separates one country from another; it marks the property limits between my neighbor and me; it tells us where the city limits are. These are examples of geographical boundaries. Just as importantly there are emotional/ psychological boundaries. It is especially important for those who come from backgrounds of rejection to establish and maintain healthy boundaries. Because these individuals are constantly seeking approval and acceptance there are apt to drop their limits with others thinking erroneously by doing this they will gain approval and acceptance. Although these behaviors are futile they continue them for what they think is a lack of alternatives. The result of this "without boundaries" lifestyle is one of being taken advantage of and often becoming part of codependent relationships. When I think of boundaries I am reminded of an incident that happened to me a few years ago while I was living in Alaska. I have always admired the huge vegetables that grew in the Matanuska Valley: carrots 18 inches long, 10 pound turnips, and the most unusual - 75 pound cabbages, large enough to easily fill a wheelbarrow! I was resolved to grow one of those gargantuan green leafy vegetables. The rich loamy soil and 20 plus hours of daylight in the summers lend itself to producing these huge crops. By early July I was well on my way to growing some really big cabbages; some were already in the 25 pound class with a month left in the growing season.

As was my habit, each morning I would water and inspect my prizes. To my shock one morning a cabbage was completely gone! Only the stalk remained, not a fragment of a leaf. Surely no one stole it, for my neighbors (scarce as they were) were not thieves. As I scratched my head I noticed a large moose footprint near the cabbage. Aha, the culprit! Although I dearly love moose, I must admit that I wished serious indigestion on the critter, or better yet, maybe I could bag him during hunting season! As I thought about it I concluded that I really couldn't blame the moose for doing what came naturally for him. Clearly, if I had placed some sort of wire fence over the cabbages I would have deterred the theft. I had not given the moose a boundary, so he took advantage of a tempting situation. Now, let us picture our lives as a garden and in it grows the things that are most precious to us: not cabbages this time, but rather family, friends, finances, and the future. Unprotected, these things can be devoured or at least trampled underfoot by uncaring people. These people are not truly our friends because they cannot be trusted to value the same things that we do. It is, therefore, incumbent upon us to place a fence around our "life's garden". However, in order not to insulate nor isolate ourselves from caring friends we must place a gate in our garden which allows access. Imagine this: One day a person comes to my home and asks if he may look at my garden. Upon scrutiny I determine that this is a person I do not trust. Should I let him in? If I want to protect the garden the answer is "no". So as to not appear mean, I may offer to allow him to look at the garden from the outside of the fence. Looky but no touchy! Next comes a person who

I trust somewhat. I escort him to the garden and we admire the crop together. I do not leave him unattended and feel secure with that approach. Next comes a dear friend who I would trust with my best hunting dog. He wants to see the garden and without hesitation I give him the keys to the gate and invite him to pick some of the crop for his use because I trust him. He has a freedom in my life that only a few do. Ingress into our lives depends wholly upon the degree of trust that we have in that person. I certainly realize that it can be difficult at first to say "no" to people that have bullied their way into our lives; but when we learn that "no" can be a good response we will then feel that we have somehow regained control over our lives. This is such a good feeling that it will motivate us to say "no" more often.

That reminds me of a story that a well-known speaker/ writer on family issues tells: It seems as though Gary had just purchased some country property in Arkansas and was there to start improving the land. He acquired a used D-6 bulldozer and although he had never driven a "cat" before he excitedly embarked on his new adventure. After a few practice runs in an open field he felt ready to head for the "tall timber" to clear some land on which to graze his horses. What a thrill it was to topple those 60 foot white pines with such relative ease. A sense of power and exhilaration was almost more than he could contain. He soon found himself knocking the trees over with such reckless abandon that in short order he had cleared about two acres. While he was wiping the sweat off his brow a pickup ground to a hurried, dusty stop in front of the dozer. A husky middle-aged, red-faced man was soon yelling at Gary," What the @#$%!! do you think you're doing??!! Gary retorted: "Clearing my land, sir, what does it look like?!" The irate man then proceeded to inform Gary that he was indeed trespassing and was clearing his land! Gary then inquired as to where the boundary markers were. The man quickly responded that the "rock over there was one marker and the other was the huge black oak over yonder". All that Gary could do at this point was hang his head and apologize profusely. Were the markers a little unclear and perhaps not legal? Surely, but the land owner did attempt to mark his property. Gary had clearly failed to even check the land plat to determine where the lot lines were. As he humbled himself and asked the man to forgive him for his careless oversight a legal battle was avoided and the men soon became friends. The man later admitted that he had wanted those mature pines harvested and that Gary had in fact done him a favor!

I'm sure we can all relate to the story and recall when we have either been the boundary breaker or had one broken. This illustrates the need for all of us to both establish our own boundaries and to respect those of others. Let's now look at the different types of boundaries.

PHYSICAL BOUNDARIES

Physical boundaries are the easiest to define for they are the ones that are most observable: highway guard rails, fences in our yards, the painted lines running down the middle of the highway, and even the walls that separate the room in our houses are all examples of physical boundaries. But how do these apply in our personal and relational lives? How do we set up physical boundaries with people and is there really a need to? These questions are almost rhetorical when we realize the result of not having physical boundaries. How many unwanted teen pregnancies could have been prevented if physical boundaries had been established? I believe another question that we all need to answer is: do we have the right to establish these limits in our lives? Of course we do! But what if we hurt the other person's feelings? What if they ditch us for setting up a physical boundary? First of all, we need to get past the feelings and just do what is the right thing. The Word of God states that obedience is better than sacrifice. By my taking literary license, that could mean that if we keep ourselves pure sexually we will not be tempted to sacrifice an innocent unborn child to the abortionist. And if you get ditched for setting a sexual boundary, thank God for it. That person was not God's choice for you!

Have you ever had a person who insists on being "in your face" when talking to you? Notwithstanding the fact that "garlic breath" may be present, one's comfort zone is at risk here. When standing and talking under normal conditions about three or four feet should separate the communicators. When seated slightly more is required. If closer than that we tend to feel uncomfortable because our comfort zone has been compromised. We can communicate our discomfort by simply moving away from the person to a more comfortable distance. Most people will take the hint. If we have been abused physically or emotionally by someone, even though we have forgiven them, we may want to set up a physical boundary, i.e., we may choose to not see them at all or limit our time with them. Some people believe that once we have forgiven a person we must give them full access to our lives again. Once again, it is a trust issue. If the offender has fully repented and has proven himself to be trustworthy then the possibility of fellowship is once again available. If not, then one has little choice but to distance themselves from that person. Another example would be if some cruel person mistreated my dear dog. I do not think that I would have them "dog sit" for me. If we have been hurt by someone and we fear that there is a distinct chance that it could happen again, let common sense prevail - set up a physical boundary, i.e. keep them away from you and what is precious to you. Remember the garden.

EMOTIONAL BOUNDARIES

These boundaries are more difficult to identify because they are more difficult to observe than physical ones. The purpose of setting emotional boundaries is to prevent ourselves from incurring unnecessary emotional injuries. Life being as it is will deal us our fair share of emotional hurts, e.g. death of loved ones, financial losses, divorces, etc. but some hurts are preventable, chief of which are in the emotional realm. Emotions can best be defined as the feelings that we all have, such as anger, jealousy, fear, anxiety, and depression, just to name a few. Although these emotions may be a natural reaction to the events of life there are precautions that we can take that will minimize their effects. Emotional upsets can nearly always be traced to an interaction with another person. We have all said at one time or another, "He or she makes me so angry!" On the surface this statement seems to be valid but closer inspection reveals that it is only a half truth. The truth is that you are angry but the falsehood is that they make you angry. No one can make you anything emotionally- mad, glad or otherwise. Yes, they can certainly influence you but the actual choice of an emotion is yours. My clients have often stated that they cannot help the way that they feel. My response is always: "Yes, you can; change the way you are thinking. Remember the progression: What you think will lead to how you feel which will lead to how you behave.

It is the responsibility of every individual to own, monitor, and change when needed, their personal emotions. We all have what we can call "individualized emotions"; ones that we have the right and responsibility to govern. Emotional distress comes when we allow others to foist their emotions on us and expect us to automatically feel the way that they do. Yes, we should empathize with the feelings of others but that in no way means that my feelings must somehow coincide with theirs. For example, a dear friend of mine is black. If he is insulted by a racial slur he will feel a certain way about it. I too will feel a certain way regarding the slur but it will not be the same as my friend's since I am not of his race. I would be empathetic but still have my individual feelings.

STICKY CODEPENDENCY

Codependency is a common condition occurring especially in marriages that is caused by the inability of the parties to separate their emotions one from the other's in a healthy manner. This lack of emotional separation is caused by the dysfunctional belief that unless we always think alike the relationship is not healthy. This is where the need for emotional boundaries becomes necessary. Emotional codependency is more easily explained than it is defined. It's like a bowl of improperly prepared spaghetti that is sticky. The pasta itself represents the particular emotions of the marriage partners. When one person's emotions are expressed, the other party automatically responds in a way that is similar to a strand of pasta when it is pulled, the other strands move as well. In a good bowl of spaghetti the strands should be able to be extracted individually without disturbing the others. In a healthy relationship one person's emotional actions should not require an exact or even a similar emotional reaction since we should be "emotionally individualistic"

While shepherding the church on Long Island I learned the secret to good spaghetti from a lady from the "old country." I complained to her one day while I watched her cooking that when preparing pasta I could never get it to not stick together. She laughed and assured me that it was easy. She then demonstrated that when the pasta was done, el dente (firm), it must quickly be placed under cold water for 15 seconds or so. This washes off the excess starch that causes the stickiness and firms up the pasta. The next secret was to douse the dish lightly with virgin olive oil which also prevents sticking. Presto! Perfect pasta! What does this have to do with codependency? Well.... The dousing of the pasta with cold water is analogous to a shocking dose of reality hitting the codependent relationship and saying "This is a sticky relationship and is not right! Things have to change." Reality also has a way of removing some of the "starch" from stubborn individuals. The olive oil poured over the pasta represents love, compassion and understanding. These act as a lubricant which reduces the friction in relationships.

The alternative to codependency is interdependency- the middle ground between independency and codependency. This is a healthy state where we do not function totally independent of the other person nor are we completely dependent upon them. If a person wanted to be totally independent of their partner why did they ever get married? Marriage is a shared relationship is it not? To be totally dependent can be compared to the child/ parent relationship which is natural in its place and time; otherwise it is unnatural and has no place in marriage. Interdependency is likened to dancing; although there is usually a clear leader, the cooperation of both parties is essential to an enjoyable dance. The time on the dance floor is fun and exhilarating but as with all good things someone has to push the pause button. Few of us can dance all night. There is then a time for a short separation when a "breather" is necessary; the lady departs to the powder room to tend to her needs and the guy checks on the ball scores. Neither partner complains about the separation for they respect each other's need for it. Interdependency relishes time together but can also enjoy time apart.

An interdependent human relationship can also be compared to the relationship that the ocean shares with the shore. Twice a day the sea comes in and kisses the shore. All the shellfish and a myriad of microorganisms under the sand of the shore rejoice for the ocean has brought in a multitude of much needed nutrients. It's feeding time and a time to revile in the wonder of the nearly invisible biological interaction between earth and sea. The ocean rejoices for it has found a stage on the shore where its roar can be heard and its waves can provide an ever changing venue for the "boys on boards." When the ocean must ebb and return to its home, the shore is not heard to cry out "please don't leave me" but rather "I'll wait for your soon return."

THWARTING MANIPULATION

Perhaps this word can be best defined as "emotional coercion." It exists especially in codependent relationships as well as other abusive ones. The chief components of manipulation are guilt and fear and once mastered they are extremely effective tools. It is unfortunate that most people who are being manipulated do not even realize it for manipulation can in most cases as subtle as a serpent. The motive of the manipulator is simply to get what they want without using physical force. However, if some manipulators cannot get what they want they may then resort to being physical. When manipulation is suspected it is vital that emotional boundaries be erected. To deal effectively with manipulation it is necessary to examine its components more closely starting with guilt. If a person can consciously get another person to feel guilty about something he can most often get what he wants from the other. Guilt is a particularly strong emotion and has caused countless myriads to do very irrational things. I have had clients (usually mothers) who continued to lavish gifts upon their children even though they were on welfare. Upon critical review it was discovered that they felt guilty about being divorced and therefore they felt that were the cause of the pain in the lives of their children. Although this was not necessarily true they believed it and that became their reality from their perspective.

We have all heard the expression "going on a guilt trip." Most people who are easily manipulated believe that going on this trip is unavoidable. This could not be further from the truth. I would like to share with you a little tool that I use frequently in my counseling practice with people who do not know how not to take guilt trips. I take a slip of 2x3 paper and write on it "Ticket good for one guilt trip. No expiration date." I then hand it to them and, of course, they accept it. I then ask them what they have just done and they look at me like a possum in the headlights and say "what do you mean?" I reply, "You just took the ticket." "Oh", they reply. I take the ticket from them, hand it back and, of course, they take it again. This is repeated perhaps 6 times or so and I finally ask them why they keep taking the ticket and they invariably tell me, "Because you gave it to me." "Did you have a choice", I say and they sheepishly reply, "Gee, I guess so." The fact finally sunk in that they were going on their "guilt trips" by their own choice. They were taking the ticket. It is a giant step forward for those in manipulative relationships to realize that they are empowered through the power of choice. No one can force them on a guilt trip; they must accept the ticket in order to go on the trip. Saying "no thank you" to the offer of a ticket is their choice.

The second device that is commonly used by manipulators to control others is fear. The Bible states that there is torment in fear and that can certainly be true in abusive relationships. *Fear of what?* Here are a few examples:

- Fear of losing the relationship, as poor as it may be. In most cases there has been a sizable investment made and who likes to lose an investment?
- Fear of losing the children. The threat of taking the kids away from someone is all too common.
- The threat of financial loss (home and investments).
- Fear of the loss of common friends due to a potential divorce.
- The fear of having to start all over again. A friend sent me the following via email today that seems to be an antidote for fear:

A basketball in my hands is worth about $19. In the hands of LeBron James it's worth $ 33 million. It depends on whose hands it's in.

A baseball in my hands is worth about $6. In the hands of Roger Clemens it's worth $475 million. It depends on whose hands it's in.

A tennis racket in my hands is good for swatting flies. In the hands of Roger Federer it's worth millions. It depends on whose hands it's in.

A rod in my hands can fend off an angry dog. A rod in the hand of Moses parted a mighty sea. It depends on whose hands it's in.

A sling in my hands is but a child's toy. A sling in David's hands became an awesome weapon. It depends whose hands it's in.

With two fish and a few loaves of bread I can whip up a tray of fish sandwiches. The same things in the hands of Jesus fed thousands. It depends on whose hands it's in.

Put some nails in my hands and I can build a bird house. Put some nails in the hands of Jesus and He produced salvation for the world. It depends on whose hands it's in.

As you can plainly see by now, it depends on whose hands it's in. So put your concerns, your worries, your fears, your hopes, your dreams, your families, your relationships, in God's hands because..... It depends on whose hands it's in. So why put your life in the hands of a manipulator when you can put it in God's hands?

SPIRITUAL BOUNDARIES

This is a subject seldom identified and rarely discussed in counseling circles because of its complexity. Although the boundaries are set up in the physical realm the effects are produced in the spiritual. For instance, when we pray we are doing something physical but something is produced spiritually because the heavenly Father not only hears our prayers but He is faithful to answer those prayers. When God hears in the supernatural area (in Heaven) He will manifest the answer in the natural area. If someone interfered with our prayers due to a lack of boundary setting, that would cause a disruption in the spiritual realm. When we attend a church or synagogue and we worship and praise God something is produced in the supernatural (spiritual) kingdom. God responds to praise, in fact, "He inhabits the praises of his people"; therefore, He may manifest Himself in the natural arena through the spiritual gifts. (See 1 Cor 12).

Let's see how the lack of spiritual boundaries in a relationship may play itself out. One's spiritual belief system is actualized in several ways. The first is through their church or synagogue. This is where they can praise and worship God, listen to the preaching of the Word, enjoy the fellowship of the saints and be edified in general. Because this is a very precious part of their life (remember the garden) it needs a fence around it, i.e. a boundary. The boundary says "do not mess with this part of my life, do not enter." To freely attend the place of worship of one's choice is a God- given right and no one has the privilege of interfering with that. And yet it is common to hear one spouse say to the other, "I don't want you going to church on Sunday; it interferes with my day", or similar remarks. The codependent person will probably "cave in" to this demand until he or she learns that their rights must be protected. Other expressions of one's faith must also be jealously guarded. This could include: private prayer time, Bible reading and meditation. If these are interfered with or controlled by others the spiritual consequences could be great.

An extreme, although real, example of violating spiritual boundaries is found in many churches. That is legalism. It can be defined as man-made rules and regulations levied upon others in an effort to produce certain desired effects or behaviors, viz. "Holiness." Although thinly veiled behind its religious cloak it is soon recognized as Satan's tool by which he will control "the laity" by the use of "the clergy." For centuries Roman Catholics were deprived of personal Bible reading because the Holy See declared that only the clergy, the priests, had the authority to read the Holy Scriptures. Clearly a spiritual boundary had been violated which caused untold damage to millions of followers. We can understand why Jesus stated in the book of Revelation that he shared a hate for the Nicolaitans. This word comes from the Greek root words "niko" which means "power over" and the word "laity" which means "common or unclean;" thus, power over the laity. Has not much of the clergy misused their authority in this way in order to gain control over the masses? This is legalism in its most defined form. It is therefore incumbent upon us all to ensure that our spiritual fences are in place so that we will not be robbed of a crop of spiritual blessings.

CHAPTER SIX

∽

TEMPERAMENT THERAPY

LIVING ACCORDING TO DESIGN

An important part of the healing process involves itself with helping the individual discover their God- given temperament. Some would use the words personality and temperament interchangeably but I believe that to be incorrect. Personality is what you allow others to see on the outside, viz. your emotional behavior. This can often be a defense mechanism, a façade or a front used to hide or disguise the real person. Temperament, on the other hand, is your actual God-given emotional predisposition which is like a set of "mind prints" that doesn't change appreciably over a life time. Temperament Therapy (TT) is helpful for anyone especially for those who have suffered from emotional damage and are struggling with self-worth and esteem issues. TT teaches us how we have been created emotionally by Our Designer and once we know our true design we can then know how to live according to that design. It's a little like taking off the old shop- worn clothes and donning our brand- spanking new "designer threads"! The Father's will is that we learn how to look and live like "king's kids" We can all put the healing garments of healthy self-value and shuck the image of damaged esteem. We need to see ourselves as we really are not as we think we are, i.e. seeing ourselves as the Father sees us!

THE TEMPERAMENT TYPES

There are five basic temperament types: **melancholic, sanguine, choleric, supine, and phlegmatic**. Everyone falls into one or more of these categories; usually we are a mixture of two or more of them. These types are like our fingerprints: we are born with these traits and they do not change appreciably over our life time. Individual temperaments may be altered somewhat by environmental influences and childhood development but the core temperament traits still remain. Let us now examine the traits of the temperaments more closely from three different perspectives: Inclusion which is social orientation and intellectual energies; Control which is our willingness to make decisions and to accept responsibility for self and or others; and Affection which is the need to express and receive love, affection, and approval and the need for deep personal relationships.

MELANCHOLIC

The Melancholic in Inclusion

1-Introverted and a loner. He is a private and serious person (this can be compounded if he is first born). To alleviate stress he needs quiet alone time every day. This quiet time will regenerate him so that he can accomplish his goals.

2-In social situations he is very selective. He approaches very few people for association and socialization. He can become stressed when pushed into social situations.

3-Task oriented. He has difficulty knowing how to relate to people so he approaches them as he would relate to a task.

4-Usually likes to work at a steady pace.

5-Self-motivated. He will not be motivated by the promise of reward or the threat of punishment.

6-Fears rejection because of low self-esteem. He searches the environment for proof that he is worthless. He is very easily offended and insulted. If rejected, he will ventilate his anger in destructive ways. He will also tend to seek vengeance.

7-High intellectual energies. He has a mind that will not shut off. He also has the ability to see pictures and images in his mind. This can cause him to re-live the past.

8-Moody. His mood swings follow his thinking process. If he thinks upward, his mood goes up; if he thinks downward, his mood goes down.

9-Distrusts people. If someone is being nice to him, he fears that they want something from him.

10-Perfectionist. He expects perfection from himself and others. The problem is that his standards are so high that no one can meet them. He is also very critical of himself and others.

11-He has a fear of economic failure.

So as not to unfairly paint a dour picture of the melancholic let us look at some of his positive traits: The biggest share of creative people, whether they are painters, sculptors, writers, or designers tend to be of the melancholic type. Because they are gifted with intellect and coupled with the desire to be alone this provides the environment in which to create. If it were not for God creating the melancholic temperament the world would probably not have enjoyed the gifts of Beethoven, Michelangelo, Renoir, or Gershwin.

The Melancholic in Control

1-Independent and self- motivated.

2-Expresses very little control over the lives and behaviors of others and will not tolerate much control over his life and behaviors.

3-Makes decisions and takes on responsibilities very well when dealing in known areas (areas previously dealt with).

4-Good leadership capabilities if he is allowed into unknown areas at his own pace.

5-He demands truth, order, reliability, and dependability from self and others.

6-If pressured into making decisions or taking on responsibilities in unknown areas he will tend to procrastinate. If he is pressured long enough, he will rebel and become angry.

7-He has a need to appear competent and in control. Fear of the unknown. When moving into unknown areas, he requires time to build up self- confidence. Others tend to see this as procrastination.

8-Becomes angry if confronted for mistakes, criticized, or made to look foolish.

9-He is legalistic, uncompromising, and rigid.

10-Becomes uneasy or anxious if he is solely responsible for anyone, including himself.

11-Will give advice when people ask, but will not pressure them to follow the advice.

The Melancholic in Affection

1-When making love, he needs little touching or foreplay. Physical expressions must lead to sex.

2-Deep relationships are few and far between.

3-Has very deep, tender feelings, but he does not feel comfortable in expressing those feelings. He rarely says "I love you".

4-He is loyal and faithful.

5-Self- sacrificing for deep relationships; he would probably give his life for his deep relationships.

6-Tends to want to live out sexual fantasies.

7-He has fear of rejection. He places the burden of proof on others because he wants to feel "safe" prior to entering into a deep relationship.

8-Devastated when he loses a deep relationship; therefore, he is cautious about developing deep relationships.

9-Becomes angry and tends to want to get even if he is hurt or rejected by a deep relationship.

10-Feels crowded or as if his "space" is being invaded if his deep relationships want to touch, hug, and kiss all the time. He prefers them to keep their hands to themselves.

11-he expresses love and affection by performing tasks, being responsible, dependable, etc.

SANGUINE

The Sanguine in Inclusion

1-Extrovert of high intensity

2-Relationship oriented. Has little understanding of tasks. He will suffer from extreme anxiety if forced to be away from other people for long periods of time.

3-He lives life at a fast pace. He is talkative and likes to be the center of attention. Has a short attention span. He will walk away from someone while they are talking when he loses interest in what is being said. It is difficult for him to pay attention in instructional setting.

4-He is motivated by the promise of reward and the threat of punishment. If he does not receive attention with good behavior he is capable of taking on bad behavior to receive attention. He also has mood swings. He is either happy or sad, and he will make the decision when to be happy and when to be sad.

5-He is very active. He finds inactivity stressful. He is highly responsive to his surroundings. A change of surroundings increases his ability to cope.

6-Highly responsive to the senses: sight, smell, sound, touch and taste.

7-He likes to shop. Shopping gives him the opportunity to be with people; however, he tends to act on impulse and spend money for thing he really does not need.

8-He is optimistic, upbeat type of person. Yesterday and tomorrow are unimportant. He is content to live for today.

9-He fears rejection. Unlike the melancholy, who withdraws from people, he tends to socialize in order to "sell himself" and gain acceptance. He will also adopt the morality of the crowd to prevent rejection.

10-Very hot- tempered, he can fly off the handle, and five minutes later forget why.

The Sanguine in Control

1-He is compulsive independent/dependent conflict. He swings like a pendulum, i.e., from needing to take on responsibilities and making decisions to being totally dependent. When he is in the dependent mode, he needs other people to control his life and make all the decisions. During this time, he is selfish and self- indulgent.

2-Tends to be driven from independent to dependent when approval is withheld.

3-When in the dependent mode, he begins to feel guilty, selfish, and worthless. These feelings cause him to swing back into the independent mode.

4-When in the independent mode, she will compulsively take on tremendous amounts of responsibility and/ or volunteer himself for projects in order to receive recognition.

5-If he does not receive the recognition he needs, he will compulsively swing into his dependent mode and stop whatever he is doing (even if it is working on an important project) and self- indulge.

6-When he draws near to burn out and the project is too much, he swings into the dependent mode (self-indulgent). This self- indulgence can be in the form of eating, taking drugs, sexual sins, drinking etc. Feelings of guilt, shame, inadequacy, and worthlessness cause him to swing back into the independent mode and the swing continues. His swings tend to intensify with age; therefore, it is possible that this trait will not be fully manifested in a youth.

7-He is weak-willed when in the dependent mode, and easily swayed.

8-When in the independent mode, he is very capable and dependable and performs with a high degree of excellence.

The Sanguine in Affection

1-Expresses and responds to a great deal of love and affection. He is uninhibited when it comes to expressing and responding to love and affection.

2-He needs to establish and maintain a deep relationship with many people.

3-Communicates by touch. If a deep relationship is hurting physically or emotionally, he will tend to want to touch them as his way of trying to uplift and encourage them.

4-He needs to receive a great deal of expressions of love and affection, i.e., hugging, handholding, kissing, and stroking. He will respond to expressions of love.

5-Fears rejection, and because of this fear, he will say and do things that he knows are not right, but will do them anyway to keep from being rejected.

6-He is very positive in regards to establishing and maintaining deep relationships. If rejected by a deep relationship, he recovers quickly and believes that if he tries harder, the relationship will work out - if not this one the next one will.

7-Adopts the morals and behaviors of others in order to meet his needs for love and affection.

8-Suffers from anxiety if not told constantly that he is loved and needed.

9-He is highly emotional. He tends to act on the emotions of the moment without thinking through the end results of his actions. If rejected he may explode in an in an outburst of anger.

10-He can be very inspiring, uplifting and loving. He has a way of making others feel loved and needed. He is like sunshine in a cloudy day.

CHOLERIC

The Choleric in Inclusion

1-He is an extrovert of a highly selective nature.

2-Appears to be people-oriented but is really task oriented. He only socializes when it is beneficial to him. He must have an agenda; otherwise he feels that it is a waste of his valuable time.

3-He is an excellent organizer in social settings. He is capable of organizing small intimate meetings as well as large corporate functions.

4-Tends to work at a fast, steady pace. It is difficult to keep up with this person.

5-Has a need to take on and organize many functions because of the need for recognition. The more recognition he receives the more he needs.

6-Appears to be open, friendly, upbeat and personable.

7-Can have a cruel abusive temper that he will use to motivate people if he cannot motivate them with his charm.

8-Associates with people he can manipulate into meeting his goals. He also tends to be critical of others when his idea of perfection is not realized.

9-He is tough-minded and strong-willed. She will usually accomplish what he sets out to do, regardless of the cost or consequences.

10-Needs recognition for accomplishments and tends to get angry if he does not receive this much- needed recognition. He is capable of doing a good job and knows it.

The Choleric in Control

1-Highly independent.

2-Makes decisions quickly.

3-Requires total control over any task that he undertakes and will tolerate little or no interference from other people.

4-Wants a great deal of control over the lives and behaviors of others but will not tolerate control over his life and behavior.

5-Has good leadership abilities. The amount of decisions and responsibilities that he is capable of would make other people cringe. Because he tends to take on too many responsibilities he is highly susceptible to burnout.

6-Is capable of undertaking poor behaviors in order to maintain control of others. He tends to associate with persons who he can dominate then ends up resenting them because they are weak.

7-Tends to be a perfectionist. Also tends to be critical of self and others especially when his standards are not met.

8-Externalizes his anger.

9-Becomes angry if someone tries to control him or tell him what to do.

10-Requires recognition for accomplishments.

The Choleric in Affection

1-Capable of expressing any amount of love and affection that he wants to express and capable of responding to any amount of love and affection to which he wants to respond.

2-Uses charm to maintain control of deep relationships.

3-Tends to develop deep relationships with people who are weak-willed then resents their weakness.

4-Has a difficult time relating to the deep tender feelings of others. He views "hurt feelings" and tears as sentimental trivia.

5-Prefers deep relationships to say: "I love you" by doing special things (tasks) rather than a lot of hugs and kisses, although he does need some hugs and kisses.

6-He rejects deep relationships if they do not meet his terms or provide love according to his standards.

7-Capable of making his loved ones feel loved, needed, and appreciated, however, he needs recognition for making them feel that they are loved... If he does not receive this recognition he will become angry and withhold his love and affection.

SUPINE

The Supine in Inclusion

1-Introvert/extrovert. He can function well either way.

2-Approaches very few people for association. He has indirect behavior. He appears to be cold and withdrawn; however, this is only a defense mechanism. He rejects others before they have an opportunity to reject him. He can be devastated when he perceives that he is not being included in social activities. Inside he is screaming: "Please include me!"

3-Relationship- oriented and task- oriented. He likes doing tasks, but they tend to stress him and wear him out (especially if he does them for long periods of time). He also likes to be with people, but they tend to stress him and wear him out (especially if he is with them for long periods of time). He needs to alternate between being with people and doing tasks.

4-He has the need to be organized, but at times, he may set aside his responsibilities to socialize.

5-He responds both to the threat of punishment and the promise of reward. He also has a need for recognition and tends to become angry if he does not receive it.

6-Because of his low self- esteem, he has a hard time accepting compliments. He has a tendency to see only his imperfections.

7-Tends to think a great deal and needs time throughout the day to think and organize or "file" his thoughts.

8-He has fear of rejection. When he feels rejected, insulted, or offended he internalizes his anger. This anger then remains unresolved. He is tenderhearted and has a gentle spirit, and so for him it is easier to say: "I am hurt" rather than: "I am angry".

9-He is moody and emotional. Crying is a safety valve that helps him deal with his stress. After a good cry, he is usually able to deal with the situation that caused the stress. A change of surroundings will refresh and energize him.

The Supine in Control

1-Tends to be dependent and a follower. He does not usually feel comfortable making leadership decisions; therefore, he prefers being a follower rather than a leader.

2-Expresses very little control over the lives and behaviors of others and needs others to take control over his life and behaviors.

3-Has a high capacity to serve people but needs to have recognition for services rendered. He tends to become angry if not recognizes for services and tend to say your feelings are hurt rather than admitting that you are angry.

4-He needs a close personal friend who will share in decision making as well as share the responsibility for those decisions.

5-He has a gentle spirit.

6-Can become anxious and stressed if he has to make decisions alone or if he must be responsible for someone other than himself.

7-Has indirect behavior. At times he expects others to know what he wants and needs without expressing the need - he wants them to read his mind.

8-He is motivated by guilt and at times he may use guilt to manipulate others into helping him.

9-He has internalized anger when he is not included in a decision concerning him. He usually does not want to be responsible for making the decision; he just wants to say that he had a part in making the decision.

10-He has a difficult time saying "no" because of his fear of rejection and of being left alone. This tends to cause him to feel used and angry.

11-He tends to be an enforcer of the rules. He needs a job where he is able to keep the rules.

The Supine in Affection

1-He requires a great deal of love and affection, and is capable of expressing a great deal of love and affection. He is a responder and usually does not initiate because he is afraid that his deep relationships may reject him.

2-At times he may feel that he is worthless and unlovable and cannot understand how anyone could possibly love him.

3-His need for love and affection often go unmet because he does not communicate them. He wants his deep relationships to read his mind and know what he wants. This is because he wants them to be genuine, however, you appear to be cold and withdrawn and your relationships think that you do not want love or affection.

4-He tends to be emotional and tender-hearted with a gentile spirit. Crying is a safety valve for him and helps him to deal with stress.

5-He expresses his love for deep relationships with words, touching, and hugging, as well as serving and performing tasks.

6-He can be easily offended, especially if deep relationships do not say "I love you" or express their love with hugs, touches and kisses.

7-He can internalize his anger and mask it as hurt feelings.

8-He has low self- esteem and a fear of being rejected by deep relationships.

9-He likes to do romantic or special things for his deep relationships

PHLEGMATIC

The Phlegmatic in Inclusion

1-He tends to relate to tasks as well as people. He likes people but has no real need to socialize; however, he can when the need arises.

2-He is best suited for tasks that require precision and accuracy, such as bookkeeping, cataloging, data entry, etc.

3-He tends to be very tough- minded and stubborn. Once his mind is made up he seldom changes it. He tends not to express his thoughts and feelings and because of this cannot tell where you are coming from.

4-He can function very well in unfriendly or hostile surroundings; in other words people do not "ruffle his feathers."

5-He has a dry sense of humor. The reason it is called dry humor is because people are never really sure whether he is serious or not. He tends to use this humor to keep people at a distance in order to keep them from draining his energy.

6-He tends to think a great deal. He has a good mind for seeing injustice and situations that need corrected. ; However because of his low energy he will try to inspire others to make the necessary changes. He feels that his responsibility ends with making others aware of the changes.

7-He is self- motivated. He will only make changes or move from the present state when he has made the intellectual decision to do so, and not before.

8-Tends to be slow- paced. He prefers working at a slow, steady pace. He may tire easily because of a low energy level. Because of the low energy he may protect what energy he has- sometimes to the point that he will withdraw from important responsibilities for a time. He tends to be an observer of life and people.

The Phlegmatic in Control

1-He is highly independent and self- motivated.

2-Tends to express very little control over the lives and behaviors of others and will allow very little control over his life and behavior.

3-Has the capability of making good decisions and delegating responsibilities to people who can handle the situations. He is also a good negotiator and peacemaker because he has the tendency to see the whole picture and is able to help people work out the details and problems.

4-Expects others to work as hard as he does to carry their end of the load. He prefers working with someone rather than working alone.

5-He tries to motivate others to take action when he is making a stand against popular opinion or sees injustice. This is due primarily to his low energy level.

6-At times he can be stubborn and rigid. He can stand his ground and no one can move him. People cannot manipulate or force him to do something he does not want to do. He tends to use his dry sense of humor to keep people from controlling him.

7-He can be overly protective of his relatively low energy reserve.

8-Tends to be an observer of deep relationships and uses his dry or sarcastic sense of humor to avoid becoming too involved. Again this can be a defense mechanism to protect his low energy reserves.

I have briefly outlined for you the pure temperament types. On the average most people are not of this pure type but rather a mix, e.g., melancholic/ phlegmatic, supine/ phlegmatic, phlegmatic/choleric etc. The blends are numerous and produce a vast array of emotional nuances. I use a very simple yet effective temperament assessment tool in my practice: The Arno Profile System. It has been used by thousands over the last 25 years or so and is considered the most accurate and user friendly version available. By simply filling out a 54 question form and having it electronically scored the client will have in their hands a very comprehensive temperament profile that is amazingly accurate (approx. 95%). Contact me if interested.

CHAPTER SEVEN

❧

THE FATHER'S LOVE

THE FATHERS' LOVE LETTER

There can be no complete or permanent healing for those who have been rejected or otherwise abused without the healing power that is only found in the love of God the Father. Over my years as a pastor/counselor I have observed countless cases concerning people who have suffered from a myriad of mental and spiritual maladies whose root cause can be traced back to either the absence of a natural father or of having a father who was in some way unloving or abusive. God's original plan was to have earthly fathers who would through their relationship with the Heavenly Father reflect His love to the children. Unfortunately, through sin, there was at some point a broken relationship between the earthly fathers and the Heavenly Father. Because of this break they were not able to reflect the Father's love; much like a broken mirror can no longer reflect light. Conversely, I have also observed children and adults who did have loving nurturing fathers and they have, for the most part, enjoyed emotionally well-adjusted lives.

There is good news, however, for the formerly abused. Our Heavenly Father in these last days is pouring out his Spirit in a fresh new way. The method by which he is doing this is found in his *Love Letter to His Children* –

THE BIBLE

Let us examine a passage found in Malachi 4:4-6. I find it interesting that this promise from The Father is found in the last words of The Old Covenant writings. There was nothing biblically penned for 430 years after this until the New Covenant writings. It is almost like God was saying that He was closing out His old letter which was a good one with a promise that soon a new letter, an even better one, was coming. It would be written about His son, Yeshua Ha Mashiach, Jesus Christ - Mal 4:4-6: *⁴Remember the law of Moses, My servant, which I commanded him in Horeb for all Israel, with the statutes and judgments. ⁵Behold, I will send you Elijah the prophet before the coming of the great and dreadful day of the Lord. ⁶And he will turn the hearts of the fathers to the children and the hearts of the children to their fathers, lest I come and strike the earth with a curse."* From scripture we know that this "Elijah" was in reality John the Baptist who came as a representation of the former possessing his type of spirit, i.e., a bold, evangelistic, fathering spirit: Luke 1:17 : *"It is he who will go as a forerunner before Him in the spirit and power of Elijah, TO TURN THE HEARTS OF THE FATHERS BACK TO THE CHILDREN, and the disobedient to the attitude of the righteous, so as to make ready a people prepared for the Lord."*

The preceding is an example of a "dualistic or repetitive prophecy", i.e., this prophecy was once fulfilled over 400 years after it was first proclaimed and it is being fulfilled today in preparation for Yeshuas' second coming. John was a voice crying in the wilderness: "prepare the way of the Lord." His preaching was raw and unvarnished. It cut to the core and was aimed toward one goal: To point the Jews who were living in utter spiritual darkness to the light of their Messiah and the salvation that comes only through Him.

As I had mentioned the Father is pouring out His love in a fresh new way. He is pouring forth His love through men he has raised up at this particular time and He has endowed these men with the heart of the Heavenly Father. These appointed/ anointed men have one task to perform, i.e. to share the Father's unconditional love with the myriad of young men and women, boys and girls who have never really known the love of a father. The love of a father is critical in the development of a child. It is the nurturing love of a mother that is vital from infancy through the age of five or six then the love of the father should take over; gently but firmly extracting the child from the comfortable nest and beginning to prepare them for the challenges of adulthood. As a major part of the child's preparation he will instruct them from the Law of Moses or the Torah. In contemporary terms this would mean teaching them from the entire Bible. As an example:

Deut. 6:
[1]These are the commands, decrees and laws, the LORD your God directed me to teach you, to observe in the land that you are crossing, the Jordan to possess,
[2]so that you, your children and their children after them, may fear the LORD your God as long as you live by

keeping all his decrees and commands that I give you, and so that you may enjoy long life.

³Hear, Israel, and be careful to obey so that it may go well with you and that you may increase greatly in a land flowing with milk and honey, just as the LORD, the God of your ancestors, promised you.

⁴Hear, O Israel: The LORD our God, the LORD is one.

⁵Love the LORD your God with all your heart and with all your soul and with all your strength.

⁶These commandments that I give you today are to be on your hearts.

⁷Impress them on your children. Talk about them when you sit at home and when you walk along the road, when you lie down and when you get up.

⁸Tie them as symbols on your hands and bind them on your foreheads.

⁹Write them on the doorframes of your houses and on your gates.

CLOSING

Well there it is, my friends. My part of the work is finished. I now place in your hands the fruits of my labors. Use these tools, given to us by our Loving Heavenly Father, with love and compassion, knowing that our labors will never be in vain. Let us never forget that Jesus was called to heal the broken- hearted. As His hands and feet are we not called to do the same? May we then go forth in the power of the Holy Spirit and bring healing to the masses that have been wounded on life's battlefield. And may God always receive the praise, honor, and glory which is all His in the name of His risen Son and our Savior, Yeshua Ha Meshiach, Jesus the Messiah.

Rev. 22:2 In the midst of the street of it, and on either side of the river, was there the tree of life, which bare twelve manner of fruits, and yielded her fruit every month: and the leaves of the tree were for the healing of the nations.

BIBLIOGRAPHY

The Holy Bible, New King James Version, copyright 1982, Thomas Nelson, Inc.

Frank Minirth, M.D., Paul Meier, M.D., Stephen Arterburn, M.Ed. *The Complete Life Encyclopedia*, 1995, Thomas Nelson Publishers

John Leonard, *Walking in Freedom*

Dr. David Seamands, *The Healing of Damaged Emotions*, 1991, Chariot Victor Publishing

Tommy Newberry, *The 4:8 Principle*, 2007, Tyndale House Publishers

Drs. Richard and Phyllis Arno, *Temperament Therapy*, 1988, The National Christian Counselors Association

Drs. Henry Cloud and John Townsend, *Boundaries*, 1999, Zondervan

Neil T. Anderson, *The Bondage Breaker*, 1990, Harvest House Publishers

Jack Stewart, *The Legalist*, 1989, New Leaf Press

Peter Lord, *Soul Care*, 1990, Baker Book House

Cleansing Stream Workbook, 1992, Cleansing Stream Ministries

John Glenn, *The Alpha Program*, 2000, Alpha Ministries

CPSIA information can be obtained at www.ICGtesting.com
Printed in the USA
LVOW132056111012

302500LV00022B/72/P